The Time Has Come

— Photo by Kaye Marvins, Houston

The Time Has Come

Gene Coulbourn Hackerman

For Adelaide

Best regards

Gene Coulbourn Hackerman

August 10, 1995

EAKIN PRESS ★ AUSTIN, TEXAS

FIRST EDITION

Published in the United States of America
By Eakin Press
An Imprint of Sunbelt Media, Inc.
P.O. Drawer 90159 ★ Austin, TX 78709-0159

ISBN 0-89015-954-8

Library of Congress Cataloging-in-Publication Data

Hackerman, Gene Coulbourn.
   The time has come : an autobiography of a Texas woman / Gene Coulbourn Hackerman. – 1st ed.
     p.   c.m.
   Includes index.
   ISBN 0-89015-954-8
   1. Hackerman, Gene Coulbourn. 2. College presidents' spouses–United States –
Biography. 3. Hackerman, Norman. 4. Rice University – Presidents. I. Title.
LC6053.H33   1994
378.1'11'092–dc20
[B]   94-38292
                                                     CIP

This book is for my four children,
each of whom I carried under my heart
and still carry in my heart —
Patricia Gale, Stephen Miles, Sally Griffith,
and Katherine Elizabeth.

"The time has come," the Walrus said,
"To talk of many things;
Of shoes – and ships – and sealing wax –
Of cabbages and kings . . . "
— Lewis Carroll

In this life I've done it all
The cabbages and kings,
The sailing ships and sealing wax
And lots of other things.

The time has come to tell you guys
What Mom is all about,
To fill in all the empty space
To let it all hang out.

I tried to do it day by day
With dignity and grace,
Sometimes I did it with panache
Sometimes fell on my face!

So here it is and as you know
Our lives were quite unusual,
I offer now what I recall
For your intense perusal.

Contents

Acknowledgment

The material for this book has been collected in scrapbooks over a period of half a century. Much of it was chronicled in Austin, Texas, newspapers by a variety of newspaper women whom I got to know quite well.

After fifty years I began to write a book and called on one of these women to show me how. Anita Howard Wukasch, a remarkable woman and a first-class newspaper writer and education editor of the *Austin American-Statesman* for twelve years, said she would be willing to lead me through the making of a book. After three and a half years of working together, I not only made a book but the best friend I ever had.

Introduction

The time has come . . . the time *has* come to tell the story of our family's life. These memoirs and anecdotes are mine, told from my perspective and experience. I do not attempt to recount the events of my husband's distinguished careers — as an eminent scientist and as the president of two of America's great universities. Norman Hackerman, of course, is a major protagonist in my story — in fact, my leading man. One of my hopes for this book is to tell the story of my life as the wife of this man and the mother of his children, but primarily, I hope it will be an honest account of one woman's journey and the way she coped with extraordinary happiness as well as extraordinary sorrows, disappointments, and fears.

First, a disclaimer. I do not speak for the network. Only for me — *my* thoughts, *my* observations and *my* participation in day-to-day living with a university. Almost forty-five years ago I started keeping notes, records, pictures and clippings for a book entitled "Me, Thee and U.T." Since then, events have been duly recorded under the title "Academia is For the Birds," which recounted my experiences at Rice University.

Part 1

Chapter 1

Staten Island

The year was 1940, the month was August, and the middle Atlantic states were as sweltering as a giant Turkish bath. My new husband drove our small black Pontiac onto the deck of the Staten Island Ferry to cross from New York City to our first home, a three-room apartment on Staten Island in a borough called Richmond. I was convinced that the toot of the horn of the ferry boat signaled the beginning of a wonderful adventure for us both. And so it did! It was the beginning of fifty years which no one could ever have imagined.

For the moment, though, Norm was working on Staten Island for the U.S. Coast Guard, waiting for some college, any college, to offer him a teaching job as a chemistry instructor. I had found a part-time job in New York. I started out at six in the morning, riding the train or bus to South Ferry, where I boarded the Staten Island Ferry (which cost a nickel) to Manhattan, then caught two trains (changing at Grand Central Station) uptown to my job with Dr. John Barclay at the Methodist Church Headquarters in New York.

Dr. Barclay called me Merry Sunshine. I was happy. My marriage was good, and I was filled with exuberance and enjoyed every day. Even the rides to work and back home were filled with stimulating reading. I finished both volumes of Carl Sandburg's *Lincoln* on the subway during the months I worked for Dr. Barclay.

He took an interest in Norm and me, and invited us for din-

1

ner at his home, high in the sky of New York in a tall apartment building. We arrived, and Dr. Barclay took us in to the living room. We chatted a few minutes, then he excused himself to get Mrs. Barclay. He brought her into the dining room, carried her to the dining room table and sat her down. She was frozen in a sitting position with crippling arthritis. I remember thinking, "Could this have been avoided if she had kept moving or exercised more? Did this have to happen to her?" She proved to be a lovely woman, and we spent a pleasant evening together.

The work with Dr. Barclay was only half-time, so I decided I should try to get another part-time job since I was in the city anyway. In the waiting room of an employment agency near Times Square, I filled out an application for every possible job I could do — stenographer, secretary, editor (my language and grammar skills were good), bookkeeper, and accountant.

The employment counselor was kind, but she didn't give me much encouragement. I had no college degree and at that time, when the country was just emerging from the Great Depression, competition was great among even college-degreed people. As I was sitting, discouraged, in the waiting room, a young woman on her way out threw a job card with a name and address on it into the wastebasket and went on out the door.

I pulled the card out of the basket. Written on it was "Dr. Walter Hager" and the notation that "Dr. Hager at Columbia University Teachers College needs a secretary. Report to Miss Dugger."

I caught a bus to Columbia University, walked into Miss Dugger's office, and told her I had come to apply for the job. Again, the subject of not having a degree came up, but Miss Dugger was going to give me a chance in the form of a battery of tests: typing, shorthand, grammar, and even a Stanford-Benet Intelligence Test. In a strange breaking of precedent, Miss Dugger told me my IQ score and said I was close to a genius! Thus, I began to work for Dr. Walter Hager, vice-president of Teachers College, for half of each day.

As I think back, I know I was extremely lucky in working with such interesting and kind people. They encouraged me to continue learning and gave me tasks that stretched my abilities.

Staten Island

After a while, I left the Methodist Church employment and filled in the other half-day with Dr. Alfred Hallquest, a professor of business administration at New York University. Dr. Hallquest was editor of *The Educational Forum,* and he did this work at his home. Again, both he and his wife, Olga, befriended me. Mrs. Hallquest, I learned, was from Texas, and I, who had never been west of the Alleghenies, was enchanted with her stories of what to me had been a land of Indians and ranches and oil. In the summers, Dr. Hallquest taught school in the College of Business Administration at the University of Texas in Austin and Mrs. Hallquest got a chance to visit her Texas family.

One of my assignments for Dr. Hallquest was to make the rounds of the New York publishing houses, picking up books for him to review for *The Educational Forum.* Once a publisher gave me a chemistry book. Dr. Hallquest said, "Let your husband review it." Norm did, and Dr. Hallquest paid him ten dollars — his first professional publication!

Another time, I showed Dr. Hallquest a poem I had written before Norm and I were married, while I was working at Johns Hopkins. He liked the poem and asked if he could publish it in the magazine. He paid me five dollars — my first appearance in print. This is the poem.

STARS

I like to think that the stars are glass,
So fragile and sparkling bright;
Just little chips from a fine, old bowl
An Angel dropped one night.

The bowl broke into a million parts,
They scattered near and far;
With bright little points and twinkling sides
Each part became a star.

The Angel, frightened by what she'd done,
Did her best to sweep them away;
So she brushed some up in a little pile
And there was the Milky Way!

Chapter 2

New York, New York

My year of working in New York City was exhilarating! I loved roaming around New York by myself, soaking up the wonderful sights and smells of all its peoples and their lives. There were men pushing long metal racks of clothes through crowded narrow streets in the garment-industry district. There were pushcarts filled with bananas, oranges, and other fruits; pushcarts displaying various articles of clothing; pushcarts holding picked-up paper and rags.

There were crowded streets and, I thought, rude people who pushed me out of their way when I stood still to crane my neck to see a bit of sky up through the tall walls of the first skyscrapers I had ever seen.

Oh yes, the smells. The smell of wonderful, sizzling hot dogs on a hot-dog stand grill, mixed with the pungent odors of pickle relish, mustard, and sauerkraut makes my mouth water even as I remember it. Sometimes, I bought one for my lunch as I went on my way to beg books from publishers for Dr. Hallquest. And there was the warming smell and taste of hot roasted chestnuts, purchased on a cold day from a street corner vendor — my dime placed in his worn woolen-gloved hand in exchange for a small warm paper sack of chestnuts placed in mine. The steps leading up to the Metropolitan Museum made a fine place to sit a moment, peel the chestnut skins off the kernels, and munch. Sometimes I had time to scoot into the museum for a brief tour.

There was the time I walked past Adele Simpson's headquar-

4

ters and offices, as I strolled along the streets of this fascinating and awesome city. "Adele Simpson," I said to myself, "Adele Simpson."

I stopped and turned back toward her brownstone. I had long admired the beautiful clothes she designed. I had never bought any because I couldn't afford them — I had not even tried any on.

However, I had done some clothes modeling at a fine department store in Baltimore, usually for the lunch crowd in the Tea Room. I had been working for Stein Bros. and Boyce, a brokerage firm downtown, and so occasionally I modeled during a lunch hour or on a Saturday. In those days, many young women did this kind of impromptu modeling work.

We got no money for it, but we did get free lunch *and,* if we liked them, the beautiful clothes we wore, for half-price!

So modeling and beautiful fashions flashed through my mind, triggered by the Adele Simpson sign on a street in New York. I turned back, climbed up the steps, walked in the door and asked for Miss Adele Simpson. I had nothing to lose.

The receptionist pushed a button and talked into a box on her desk and then said, "You may go through that door."

I went through the door and stood facing an attractive dark-haired woman who stood up and invited me to sit down. I was quite a bit taller than she — she was almost what the fashion world calls "petite."

Miss Simpson and I visited for a while and I asked her if she could possibly use me as a model from time to time. She smiled kindly and told me she designed clothes for short women only!

Chagrined, I smiled too, thanked her, and rose to leave.

"Please sit down," she said. I sat down again and waited. "You have a lovely smile," she continued, "you could really do some modeling for another fashion house that designs for taller women. I have a friend who heads up the biggest modeling agency in the country. Perhaps you have heard of him. His name is John Robert Powers."

Had I heard of him? My jaw dropped. This couldn't be true — my sitting in Adele Simpson's office, talking about John Robert Powers in New York City!

5

The Time Has Come

While I struggled to regain some semblance of composure, Miss Simpson pulled a sheet of notepaper toward her and said, "I am writing a note of introduction to him for you. Take it to his office and tell him I sent you. I'll call him and tell him you're coming." And she gave me Mr. Powers' address!

This stunned young woman thanked her profusely, over and over, and glided out the door, down the steps, and on to the office of the great — the one and only — the guru of the fashion world — *the* John Robert Powers!

Believe it or not, the great man actually saw me, invited me into his office, talked to me for about ten minutes, then asked me to walk across the room, turn around and walk back, then repeat. Then he asked me to sit down again.

"My dear young lady," he said, "You would not photograph well, your face is not bony. However, Adele is right. You have a lovely smile. You would be great on the runway presenting new fashions to buyers."

He stopped, turned his chair toward the window and looked out for a minute or two. Then he turned back toward me and said, "I can offer you that kind of job which will pay fifteen dollars an hour. You would need to lose ten pounds first."

I said, "Thank you, Mr. Powers. I will go home and talk it over with my husband."

He said, "Fine," and we shook hands and said goodbye.

Once I reached the street, I skipped along, grinning and pinching myself to see if I were awake. The trip from Manhattan to Staten Island was *interminable*.

I rushed into our apartment, grabbed Norm and shouted, "I have a job offer for fifteen dollars an hour!"

Since this was an unheard of wage in 1941, Norm said, "Doing what?" I filled him in on all the details of my wonderful, exciting, unbelievable day.

"And all I have to do," I said, "is lose ten pounds."

He looked at me, and then he said, "I like you the way you are."

I called Mr. Powers the next day, thanked him very much and regretted that I couldn't take the job. My husband liked me the way I was!

New York, New York

*   *   *

Sunday mornings in New York were grand. Memories, memories — they, like the events which produced them, occurred in certain time slots in my mind. Those I have already recounted occurred on weekdays as I became involved in the various jobs I managed to hold during that year in New York City.

The memories I hold most dear are of the weekends Norm and I got to spend together. We had been married only a month, and living together was a new experience.

The 1940 World's Fair had been built in New York at Flushing Meadows (now the home of the U.S. Open tennis matches). We spent many Saturdays walking hand-in-hand through the thousands of wonderful displays and exhibits at the fair. Sometimes, we took a lunch and bought a soft drink there to wash our sandwiches down.

I remember distinctly the General Electric exhibit, where Norm expressed his ideas on something called a computer. There was something (perhaps an early voice-programmed computer) called "Pete-the-Voder," which said, "How are you?" with all the diphthongs hanging out! "Haoo-aher-ooo!" I would remember Pete vividly twenty years later, when Norm brought the first computer to the University of Texas campus!

Sometimes we would see a show at the fair. The one I remember best was a performance by Gypsy Rose Lee. This statuesque brunette was a high-class stripper. My very new husband assured me I wanted to see the show; and in we went. (I had never been to a burlesque show.)

When the theatre was full, the lights dimmed, the music began and the spot shone on a fully clothed Miss Lee. Very genteelly she removed a glove and tossed it into the audience, then moved gracefully for a few minutes to the music. Then she slowly removed the other glove and followed the same graceful procedure. At all times the bright spotlight followed her every move. With the slow, sensual one-by-one removal of pieces of clothing and the pulsating music, the gently swaying Miss Lee had moved much of the audience to fever pitch, some shouting, "Take it off — take it all off!"

7

The Time Has Come

This brand-new bride, her face the color of fire, prayed for Miss Lee to leave something on!

As the drumbeat increased and the crowd applauded, the lady reached to untie the last bow holding a covering garment — and all the lights went out!

When they came back on, she was gone! "Now, *that*," I thought gratefully, "is *class*."

*   *   *

Sundays were such special days for us that 1940–41 year. Sometimes we explored Staten Island from tip to tip. I had my first pizza in a place called a pizzeria. It was an Italian restaurant with wooden tables and checked tablecloths. At one end was a huge brick oven with a large, flat wooden shovel. The circles of dough, thin and flat, with their toppings of tomato sauce, cheese, onions, green pepper and pepperoni were shoved into the brick oven on the shovel, carefully shaken off the shovel, and removed, after baking, on the same wooden shovel! Wine, salad and spaghetti were also served.

We met a couple there, Anita and Abe Berman. They were young and childless like us, and we shared an interest in tennis. We sometimes played on Sunday afternoons together, ending a warm, friendly day at the pizzeria.

Most of all, I loved our Sundays in the city itself. Downtown New York was a ghost town on Sunday.

Norm and I spent many Sunday mornings taking the ferry to the base of Manhattan, South Ferry. We then walked from South Ferry up Wall Street drinking in the beauty of the buildings reaching higher in the sky than any I had ever seen. Then, cradled at the base of them, the lovely little fence-enclosed church, circled by a small plot of grass inside the fence — the Church of The Holy Trinity.

We held hands as we strolled along deserted streets, stopping usually at an open-faced diner where we ate wonderful pancakes drenched with Log Cabin maple syrup. As we sat on stools at the counter and drank our coffee, we decided what we would do that day in the city.

New York, New York

Sometimes, we went to the Bronx Zoo. We would ride the elevated trains high over the streets below, passing upper stories of crowded apartment houses and feeling like voyeurs looking into glass windows barely three feet away.

Sometimes we rode the double-deck bus up Fifth Avenue and on to Central Park and had snow cones from a vendor in the park.

Once we rode a hansom cab with its top down around the park. We walked a lot those Sundays and at the end of the day, tired but happy, rode back to South Ferry on the subway, caught the ferry home to Staten Island, picked up our little car, and drove home.

Only once did we invite a guest to dinner.

When I left Stein Bros. to marry Norm, my friends there threw a wedding shower for me. Because I was moving to New York, my boss wrote to the office there asking that they extend every courtesy.

When I arrived in the city, I called Miss Davis, who was the administrative assistant to the manager. She knew who I was and kindly asked me to lunch. After lunch, we returned to their office at the New York Stock Exchange building. The office was one of those above the big stock exchange floor and had a small balcony. By stepping out I could see the bustle and hear the noise of the stock market trading.

Miss Davis said, "Women are not allowed on the floor of the exchange."

"Why not?" I asked.

"They just aren't," she said.

"Not even one foot?"

"Well, all right," she said.

So we sneaked down the hall stairs, opened a door which said "keep out," and I stuck my foot through the door and planted it firmly inside the Exchange floor! Miss Davis and I giggled like schoolgirls and I invited her to dinner next Sunday.

I spent the next Sunday cooking for Sunday dinner. It was an elaborate menu including appetizer, meat, vegetables, salad, and a beautiful baked whole cauliflower sprinkled with grated cheese and bread crumbs.

9

The Time Has Come

Dinner was a success. Miss Davis said so. We took her to the ferry, went home and washed the dishes.

A week later Miss Davis wrote a lovely thank-you note. Two weeks later I returned home on a very warm evening and the stench was awful. Locating the smell, I yanked open the oven door. There sat the beautiful, baked cauliflower which I had forgotten to serve! It had slowly rotted apart.

*   *   *

In the spring of 1941, Norm and I went to Atlantic City to a meeting of the American Chemical Society. He had his resumé in hand and stayed near the convention employment desk, where companies and universities from throughout the nation were recruiting young chemists. Hallelujah! He was offered a teaching position at Virginia Polytechnic Institute with the rank of assistant professor.

So in September 1941, we moved to Blacksburg, Virginia, and at twenty-four I began my life as the wife of an academic man. I said goodbye regretfully to the Hallquests and Dr. Hager, and the two of us headed toward Virginia in our little Pontiac coupe, so proud to finally be "Dr. and Mrs. Norman Hackerman, assistant professor of Chemistry, Virginia Polytechnic Institute, Blacksburg, Virginia!"

Chapter 3

Blacksburg, Virginia

lacksburg, Virginia. Virginia Polytechnic Institute. When I think of Blacksburg and the three years we lived there, I am caught in a montage of quickly changing, kaleidoscopic images and emotions — mountains and snow, gorgeous springs, Pearl Harbor, Pat's birth, friends whom I would miss until this day, lipstick on my towels left by thoughtless girls, Norm gone on a secret mission, loneliness, and a telephone number for the YMCA in New York.

But let's sort it all out and try to make sense of that time fifty years ago. When we arrived in Blacksburg in September 1941, the leaves of the maples and oaks were beginning to turn and the days were crisp and the nights cool. For a time we lived in a small duplex apartment, but were on the list for a faculty apartment, which opened up within a few weeks. This new apartment was on the fourth floor and had dormer windows that reached almost to the floor and provided a stunning view of the campus with its changing seasons. Our apartment actually was converted from two apartments, so we had to go out into the hall to get to the bedroom. A glass enclosure, ceiling to floor, wall to wall, cut off that unnecessary stairwell.

VPI, the A&M of Virginia with a military corps, had an all-male student body save for a few dozen women students, mostly daughters of faculty members, who were enrolled in the Home Economics Department. The men students wore uniforms of gray with a cape buttoned back and lined with red. On snowy

11

mornings, I opened the dormer windows so I could hear them singing as they marched to class and see the grays and reds of their uniforms dotting the white hillside. Tears spring to my eyes now remembering the young men of Virginia Polytechnic, uniformed and marching, readying, I suppose, for a war we didn't really believe would happen. And yet it did come, and many of these boys would go and never return. Remember, this was Virginia and memories of the old Confederacy lingered. Defending your country was expected.

I became involved in faculty life, made friends with the wives of the young faculty, and volunteered the two of us to be chaperons for cotillions and Germans. We opened our home to young women from Virginia women's colleges who were invited for weekends of dancing and partying. I remember my amazement that the girls wiped their lipsticks on my white towels . . . and never wrote "thank-you notes" for providing a place to stay!

Our first child, Pat, was born in Blacksburg. We had wanted a baby for a long time, and Pat was awaited with joy and greeted with love. Norm was with me when she was born, but soon he left and would not return until she was eighteen months old.

December 7, 1941, was my twenty-fourth birthday. To celebrate, Norm took me to Roanoke, thirty-five miles from Blacksburg. We had lunch at the beautiful Roanoke Hotel Dining Room, built in the shape of a roundhouse by the Norfolk and Western Railroad. After lunch we went to a movie. Suddenly, the sound ceased, and a man came out on the stage and told us that the Japanese had dropped a bomb on Pearl Harbor. The theatre lights came on, and a stunned and silent audience filed slowly out into the afternoon sunshine. We climbed into our little car and drove back to Blacksburg through the winding roads and the gathering dusk.

Norm enlisted in the navy, where he would have the rank of lieutenant (jg). The day he signed up, he ordered his shoes and was measured for a uniform. He still has the shoes, but the uniform order was canceled. Virginia Polytechnic was an army school, the home of an Army Special Training Program. The powers that were had decreed that Norm should stay at VPI, to help train engineers and scientists to go to the Pacific to build airstrips, I suspect, among other things. Pat was just three months old when Norm told me he was going to "work for the government" in New York, for Kellex Corporation. I had the address of the YMCA where Norm was staying, and a telephone number. But we didn't have money for many long distance calls. Travel was restricted, so for fifteen months Norm and I stayed together by mail. I knew nothing about what he was doing, and only after the war, after the atom bomb was dropped, did I learn that he had been working on the atom bomb!

After Norm went to New York, I began working half-days for Dean Norton of VPI's College of Engineering. Dean Norton had come from Bozeman, Montana, and was an industrial engineer and a specialist in time and motion studies.

"What are 'time and motion' studies?" I asked him.

"It's the reason paper towels are hung high up in restrooms," he answered. "Our studies show that people use fewer towels when they are hung high than when they are lower." (The water runs down into their sleeves!) I knew he was joking, and that the idea was to do jobs more efficiently — less time, less cost.

One day Dean Norton announced to me that an eminent visitor was coming to VPI — the most famous of the time and motion researchers, Dr. Frank Gilbreth, and his wife, Lillian, also an expert in the field.

Dr. Norton asked me to "look after" Mrs. Gilbreth while he and her husband met with faculty and students in seminars. This encounter changed my life.

As she and I sat chatting over a cup of tea, Mrs. Gilbreth let drop the stunning information that she had twelve children, as well as a taxing career and a large home to run.

"How do you get it all done?" I asked.

"By the efficient use of time," she said. "The next time you make a bed, see how long it takes you; when you wash dishes, check on your efficiency."

I did this, and found that I could, by moving fast and concentrating, cut my bed-making time down two minutes. The same was true of dishwashing. By working more efficiently, I could cut the time this took in half. But that wasn't all Mrs. Gilbreth taught me that day.

13

The Time Has Come

"For heaven's sake," she said, "don't waste time soaking in a hot bath. You are indulging yourself. Take a shower. You can get just as clean in a shower, in a quarter of the time. Actually one to two minutes!"

"Find ways to do everything fast and well. Don't dawdle. Get up and get things done."

So that's what I have done for fifty years, and the time I have saved by following Mrs. Gilbreth's advice has made possible endless hours of learning, fun, and through volunteering, helping in the various communities in which I have lived.

When my four children were in school, the time and motion benefits were most noticeable. One of my friends remarked, "Gene, how do you do it? By nine, you have four kids delivered at schools, beds made, dishes washed, supper ready, and you have all day — until you pick the children up in midafternoon — to do whatever you want to do. Amazing."

Of course, during those early days I was lonely for Norm, and sorry that he couldn't see Pat in all her wonderful baby stages of sitting up, walking, beginning to talk and being the best that Norm and I could have produced.

So what did I do with my time? I began three activities which through the years I have continued in one way or the other — illustrating, teaching, and home design. I am the eternal amateur, but an enthusiastic amateur, and I have yet to say, "I can't do that." I'll take on any challenge, but admit to falling on my face sometimes when I do!

One of my best friends at VPI was Carolyn Norton, Dean Norton's daughter, and one of the two dozen women students on campus. Carolyn asked me to teach her to type. I thought, "Why not get several young women together and set up typing classes? I can teach six as easily as one."

So we did. Three nights a week after supper, I met with six young women in the College of Engineering, setting up typewriters borrowed from the secretaries' desks. My students paid me one dollar a session, which netted me eighteen dollars a week. (Three nights, six girls.)

My willingness to try anything came when Dean Norton asked me to draw some simple cartoons to illustrate a teaching

14

instruction booklet he had written. Remember, this was wartime, and drawing and painting supplies were not to be had in Blacksburg. The bookstore did sell India ink for strictly line drawings, but what to do for shading?

By chewing wooden matchsticks at the end, I was able to make a pretty good substitute for a brush — dipping the fragmented parts in ink and shading the drawings.

Pat gave me an opportunity to do my first home design. Our apartment was small, but I rearranged it for Pat's nursery. I bought pale pink net polka-dotted material and made curtains for the nursery and a matching coverlet for the baby's bed.

Remember the dormer windows that had given me so much pleasure when I first arrived in Blacksburg, as I gazed at the changing scenery? These windows became a problem with a toddler. Pat might walk right out of the fourth floor and fall to the ground below!

I bought picket fencing three feet high, installed it across the dormer windows' sills and placed pots of blooming plants between the fence and the windows. Pat was the only little girl in Blacksburg with a flower garden in her room.

It was spring again in Blacksburg, and the telephone rang and Norm had some news for us. That old black magic of the Atlantic City convention had worked again! He had been offered an assistant professorship at the University of Texas at Austin — did I want to go? I encouraged him to take the job, and he says to this day I *made* him come to Austin.

Chapter 4

Early Austin

Dr. Roger J. Williams is the biochemist who discovered the B vitamin pantothenic acid. Dr. Henry Henze developed the anti-convulsion drug that has saved the lives of many epileptics. These two great men interviewed Norm at the 1944 meeting of the American Chemical Society in Atlantic City and offered him a job as an assistant professor at the University of Texas at Austin.

When Norm called to tell me about this offer, my enthusiasm surprised him. "I think you should take it," I said. Pat was eighteen months old, and most of her life she and I had been alone in Blacksburg while Norm was working in New York City. Now we would be together as a family. Before we could leave, I needed to pack up the baby, the baby buggy and our personal items to go in the car, and make arrangements to have the furniture moved to Roberdeau Storage in Austin until we could get there and claim it.

After getting all this attended to, Pat and I met Norm at his parents' house in Westminster, Maryland, to say goodbye to them. We also stopped in Baltimore to say goodbye to the only family I had there, my brother, John, and his family. About December 28, we headed for Austin in our little black Pontiac. Our suitcases were stacked on the floor behind the front seat. We stacked them to be level with the back seat so that we could lay the crib mattress on top of them. On top of this mattress was an eighteen-month-old baby in a pink snowsuit, snaps in the crotch, and her adorable face surrounded by the snowsuit's hood.

16

Early Austin

It was wintertime, and we were crossing snow-capped mountains, trying to keep ourselves and the baby warm.

As we drove through the Blue Ridge Mountains of Virginia, I filled several shopping bags with wet diapers. Leaning over the back of the front seat, I seemed to be changing diapers all day long. I really appreciated those snaps in the snowsuit crotch!

Of course, there were no disposable diapers in those days. At night, in the tin showers of the motels we stayed in, I washed the diapers and dried them in front of gas heaters.

The Pontiac's windshield wipers were great for rain, but were no match for the thin film of ice constantly forming on the windshield. As Norm concentrated on the driving over the icy mountain roads, the lady in the passenger seat of the car had the pleasure of scraping ice off the windshield with a razor blade during frequent stops!

We crossed the Mississippi at Memphis, with the big river at flood stage from melting snow. We were in a creeping line of cars with water washing up almost to the doors of the Pontiac. I was afraid we wouldn't get across. But we finally made it into West Memphis, to Arkansas, then turned southwestward toward Texas and Austin.

Much of the trip is a blurred memory. I remember that Norm had to concentrate on the unfamiliar highways and hazardous driving conditions. In Baltimore, a sign in the streetcars said, "Do not disturb the motorman." Norm believed this admonition held for the driver of an automobile, too, so we engaged in no pointless conversation. I can't remember the motels or even the towns we stayed in. I do remember giving the baby crackers and bottles whenever she was hungry, and the incessant changing of diapers. I do remember Arkansas' pot-holed roads, the dismal huts, and the run-down farms, and that I began to wonder about this West that I had never seen.

New Year's Day we left the ice and snow and flood waters behind us. We drove into Austin, coming in on the Old Dallas Highway, which is now Lamar and Guadalupe. It was January 1, 1945, and the sun was shining. The highway was divided by a lovely broad esplanade. The grass was green in this center island, green leaves were on the trees, and the sky was a sparkling sapphire.

17

The Time Has Come

I took that pink snowsuit off that baby, turned to Norm, and said, "This is it, Bub! I'll never leave Austin, Texas," and I didn't for twenty-five years. And I only moved to Houston then.

We checked into a small, cheap motel in the four thousand block of Guadalupe, across the street from the Austin State Hospital, and stayed there for two or three weeks (still washing those wet diapers in a motel shower). The night of our arrival, we took the baby and headed for the Piccadilly Cafeteria at Eighth Street and Congress Avenue, where we had our first dinner in Austin, Texas — our new hometown.

When Norm went to the Chemistry Department the next day, he found that he would be sharing an office with Al Matsen. Al and his wife, Ceil, were hospitable and friendly. They invited us to dinner, and their little boy, Ricky, and Pat were happy friends. I have a snapshot of Ricky and Pat playing in a sandbox in the Matsens' backyard. Over the years to come, Ceil and I would become very close friends.

Dr. William Felsing was chairman of the Chemistry Department. The Felsings, who had two teenagers, occasionally invited us to their home for dinner and always said, "Bring the baby." I began to understand why Austin was known then — and still is — as "the friendly city."

Our first home-like living arrangements were in the home of Dr. and Mrs. Clarke Cleveland, eleven blocks north of campus. Dr. Cleveland was a professor of mathematics and Mrs. Cleveland was an artist. We had a small living room, larger bedroom, and tiny bath. To shut the bathroom door, one had to go all the way into the room, turn around, then close the door. But I have always liked small bathrooms — partly because of the advice long ago from Mrs. Gilbreth, who believed too much time was wasted in tub soakings. We stayed two months with the Clevelands, long enough for Pat and Mrs. Cleveland to form a fast friendship. Pat called her Grandma. The Clevelands were generous to share their home with us, but remember, this was the end of wartime when it had become a usual occurrence to make room for young families. It also was a time of increasing rents because of the many GI Bill students coming to the university and the hiring of more faculty.

18

Early Austin

Ceil Matsen helped me find an apartment at the corner of West Avenue and 34th Street. It was a second-floor apartment with a porch opening off it and cost seventy-five dollars a month, a large bite out of Norm's $200-a-month income. By that time, I had begun supplementing Norm's university salary by typing theses and dissertations for Martha Ann Zivley on a table in the living room. We had no rugs. The woman living downstairs had migraine headaches and my typing bothered her, so I moved my work station to another room.

My love of the University of Texas was instant. I was invited to join, as were all faculty wives, the University Ladies Club. The University Ladies Club had an active Newcomers Group. Eager to become a part of the university and Austin communities, I went to every activity of the Newcomers — bridge, book reviews, drama, music. My oldest (in terms of knowing them) Austin friends came from the women I met during those first few months — Betsy Watt, Sylvia Lester, Ceil Matsen, Jean Maurer. We were a mixed bag! Our husbands were in different disciplines — two were chemists, one was an English teacher, one taught in the art department, and one was an engineer. All were young and all were assistant professors.

The five of us each had one child, except Sylvia, who had two. We often took care of each other's children when one or the other of us needed to run errands. For example, Pat stayed with Sylvia Lester while I went house-hunting. In return, I wallpapered Sylvia's kitchen. She and I still remember the ivy patterned, green and white wallpaper I pasted laboriously on her kitchen walls (which later were inside Mike and Charlie's Restaurant).

The five of us were just the ideal number for the kind of nursery school we planned. Our scheme was that each of us would take care of all the children one morning a week, thus freeing four of us each day for our own pursuits, like taking classes at the university or pursuing various projects, like wallpapering or grocery shopping.

This wasn't going to be an ordinary nursery school. We wanted to do it right. So we called Lucille MacCorkle, past director of the University Nursery School, and invited her to come

19

over for a cup of coffee and to tell us how to deal with these children. She gave us child development tips that were invaluable, reminding us that two- and three-year-olds have short attention spans and that new activities must be waiting for them every fifteen minutes or so. We fell into a nine-to-noon routine: play, a cracker, a story, juice, more play. Our class consisted of Paul Lester, Joanna Maurer, David Watt, Ricky Matsen, and Pat Hackerman.

Looking back, I realize the magic of those early days and how rich we were in those friendships. Ceil took care of Pat when Steve was born, and I held her hand when her second baby, Megan, was born. We gave each other Toni waves. We made costumes for our children's first performances — in ballet, in tumbling, for Halloween. We talked about ideas and children, how we could stretch the money, new recipes.

This group was unique — we never gossiped! By some instinctive magic, none of us said an unkind word about anybody.

We attended Newcomers for the two years we were allowed to, and I grew to care deeply for my four friends with the small children. As we shared each other's first-borns, I grew to care for those children, too. As we could no longer attend the art group, drama group, music group, sewing group, and so on, I asked the other four to come to my house to sew. They did, we did, and the Sewing Club was formed! I had moved to Sharon Lane and the five of us met there. The Sewing Club continues to this day. During the fifteen years we lived in Houston, I came back to Austin whenever I could to visit the Sewing Club.

We have all had our triumphs and our sadnesses, not the least of which was the shared sadness when Betsy Watt died. I fell apart when she died. I miss her still.

Jean Maurer's death was another shared grief, and I was then living away from Austin and could not be near.

The Sewing Club continues. Now we talk about grandchildren and our projects, and how lucky we have been to have each other.

Chapter 5

Sharon Lane

A home of one's own. I have felt as long as I can remember that every person in America should own a piece of land — a piece of his or her country, state, town. Since we felt at home in Austin immediately — Norm at the university and I in the community, we felt the sooner we could buy a house, the better it would be for our family.

If a person or a family plans to stay anywhere a year and half or longer, it is a much wiser use of money to buy than to rent. U.S. tax laws are set up to benefit the homeowner. So in the summer of 1945, pregnant, and without any money for a down payment, I went house hunting.

The summer of 1945 was ghastly. This was my first Texas summer. The heat was more intense than I had experienced before. The nursery school my four close friends and I had formed provided good care for Pat four mornings each week while real estate agents drove me around Austin. I saw many houses in all parts of the city. Most were overpriced because of the influx of more teaching personnel to accommodate the veterans coming to the university to take advantage of the GI Bill.

After much looking, I found a large, seventy-five- by two-hundred-ten-foot piece of land with forty-eight trees — beautiful live oaks — on Sharon Lane in Tarrytown. But it had no house. Its only building was a well-built garage apartment at the back of the lot, with handsome hardwood floors and excellent millwork throughout. A contractor had built the garage apartment for his daughter, who had planned to live there until a house was built in front.

I could see all sorts of possibilities. The children — I was already counting Steve who hadn't been born yet — could sleep in one room for a while. Norm went with me to see it with his usual disinterest in houses.

The price was $6,000 for a livable building plus an enormous lot with grass and trees in one of the newer residential areas of Austin.

The down payment was $1,500 — money we didn't have. Norm and I went to the Capital National Bank in downtown Austin to ask to borrow the money. Norm did the talking.

"What do you have for collateral?" asked the banker.

Norm's short temper got shorter.

"If we had collateral, we wouldn't be asking for a loan," said he. "Why in the hell would we be asking to borrow money if we had any?" Norm got up and left. I followed him out.

So where could we find money?

Dr. Henry Henze, who had interviewed Norm for the chemistry job at the university, and his wife Elizabeth were mentors to us both. From some comments Elizabeth had made to me, I felt that Dr. Henze was eager to keep Norm at the university. So I got up my courage and asked Dr. Henze if he would lend us the money to make the down payment. He did, and we signed a note for a prescribed time to repay with interest.

We made the mortgage payments along with paying off the Henzes. At the end of three years, we made the last Henze payment. We invited them to come to the house, and we burned the note in the fireplace. It was a happy occasion, a tribute to us all and our friendship.

To the primary mortgage we added another mortgage to add a living room onto the house. Workmen were still building this addition when we moved in about six weeks before Steve was born.

The living room was attached to the front of the house, where the kitchen window looked out over the front lawn. As the carpenters were banging around in the new addition, I borrowed some boards from them to put across the banisters on the stairway leading to the bedrooms upstairs. I stood on these boards to paint the second-story ceiling over the stairwell. I used Kemtone, a water-based paint that can be wiped up easily. I painted with a large brush attached to the end of a broomstick. I didn't see anything unusual about this. However, the carpenters seemed a little distraught and kept leaving their own work to come where I was painting to check on me.

"Lady, please get down from there," one of them said. "We don't know how to deliver a baby."

But Dr. Morris did.

Steve was born a few days later — November 21, 1945. Dr. Truman Morris in those days scheduled births, so he decided when was the best time for me to have the baby.

Steve was our Thanksgiving child. I remember still the beaming of my entire self — the elation I felt because of this beautiful child Norm and I were fortunate enough to have produced. It was just about that time that I realized these children, Pat and Steve, were gifts from God. God blesses us with babies, I believe, so that we may experience the only true, unselfish love. Parents give love, expecting nothing in return, but the baby, miracle of all miracles, gives us back that love a thousand times over.

In those days a mother stayed in the hospital for two weeks, "regaining her strength." During this time, Ceil and Al Matsen kept Pat, with Norm looking in on her every day.

Ceil has a photograph of Norm and Al building a fence around a sand pile where Pat and the Matsens' little boy, Ricky, played. Norm had some other housekeeping experiences while I was in the hospital. One day he came in waving the bill from Southern Union Gas Company.

"Why didn't you pay this bill?" he fussed. "I had to send them a check!"

This bill and the check I had sent before going to the hospital apparently had crossed in the mail. The gas company and I straightened it out after I got home.

During my time in the hospital, Austin's first blue norther of the season blew in. Our upstairs bedroom at Sharon Lane was cold, and Norm complained about that. He said he couldn't sleep for being cold. I suggested that he put newspapers under the mattress to keep the bed a bit warmer.

When Steve and I went home from the hospital, we had a German woman stay for two weeks to help me with the baby and do the housework. This was the woman's career — to help young mothers with their new or added responsibilities. She was a kind of itinerant practical nurse, adapting every few weeks to a new situation and new people.

Steve's first pediatrician was a young woman with a small child. I remember she made house calls when Steve had a particularly rugged bout with asthma. At the time I marveled at her dedication to both her work and home.

As soon as the household was more or less back to normal, I continued my building of the house on Sharon Lane. This construction project went on for twenty-five years, adding and improving, building and sawing, hammering and wallpapering. Our three-room garage apartment with one bath at the end of twenty-five years had become a thirteen-room house with four bathrooms and a quarter century of wonderful living for our family of six.

About halfway through this building project, eleven years after we moved into the garage apartment, a newspaper article appeared about the house. The article follows:

AUSTIN AMERICAN-STATESMAN
Sunday, October 21, 1956

FORMER 3-ROOM GARAGE APARTMENT
NOW 9-ROOM HOME FOR HACKERMANS
By Lois Hale Galvin

The big, rambling nine-room house on 2000 Sharon Lane was just a three-room garage apartment back in 1945 when it became the home of the Norman Hackermans.

Its topsy-like growth over the intervening eleven years is due primarily to Mrs. Hackerman's ingenuity with a paint brush, wallpaper and a sewing machine, plus an uncanny skill in "home-building know-how."

The very attractive mother of three children and a coed at the University of Texas, where her husband, Dr. Norman Hack-

Sharon Lane

erman, is Chairman of the Chemistry Department, Mrs. Hackerman is a woman whose initiative and careful planning have achieved an adequately spacious home radiating friendliness and family contentment.

Inside and out, the house aptly expresses Mrs. Hackerman's philosophy of a home: "A place of peace and security for our family; hospitality for our friends."

On Shaded Lot

The L-shaped house is located at the back of a tremendous tree-shaded lot, most of which is a beautifully kept lawn. A long pink cement block walk leads from the street gate to a matching terrace in the L-shaped area, which Mrs. Hackerman built with the help of her half-day-a-week yardman. In the L of the house is a small, roofed porch with square columns, all in white, set against two walls of narrow white siding. The effect of this white arrangement against the gray exterior of a textured asbestos shingles and white trim of the house is a traditional look, further enhanced by a low white fence enclosing the terrace.

The fenced terrace, like most of the additions, was the outgrowth of a family need. The terrace was enclosed to make a safe play area for three-year-old Sally, when she was a toddler. She's now a member of the nursery school set, and brings home her share of classroom accomplishments to be placed on the playroom wall for family approval along with those of her teenage sister, Pat, and eleven-year-old Steve.

First Project

The playroom, which also serves as a family room, was originally the double garage, and was the first remodeling project Mrs. Hackerman tackled. With the aid of a University student at thirty-five cents an hour, she divided the garage with a center wall and a ceiling of wallboard and sheetrock. He held the boards while she nailed them in place.

Since that time all of the garage has been remodeled into a cozy room that's served in turn as a playroom, bedroom, then back to a playroom. Another garage added on when the first one was usurped for other purposes has also undergone an overhauling, and is now Dr. and Mrs. Hackerman's bedroom, where a spacious area is devoted to his work desk.

The Time Has Come

A portable canopy carport now houses the family car, and has reached the expanding limitations of the lot.

Sharing the downstairs area with the garage was a huge family-sized kitchen that included the dining area. The garage and kitchen were separated by a small entrance and walled stairway leading to the two upstairs bedrooms and bath. Mrs. Hackerman did the paperhanging in this area herself, including the two-story high ceiling.

Draw All Plans

Since that time she has become quite proficient in every phase of remodeling and redecorating projects. She first draws up plans for every job, figures the amount and kind of materials needed and estimates the cost. She has made all of the financing arrangements, repaying the cost from her house allowance.

Also, she does her own contracting for each specific phase of work, carpenter, plumber, electrician, etc., and supervises the construction, doing much of the actual work herself, especially the painting and paperhanging.

Modernizing the kitchen was her latest project. Although one of her long cherished dreams was to have a sink high enough for a tall woman, which she is, and a built-in stove unit and wall oven, she never got around to installing these until her daughter, Pat, finally coaxed her into it.

With all of its new modern equipment and inlaid brick-design linoleum that extends to the breakfast area, the small entrance hall, and the adjoining dining room, the kitchen still retains its cozy atmosphere.

Economy Necessary

Economy was a necessary requisite in all of her remodeling and redecorating plans, especially at first when her husband was a $200-per-month assistant professor at the University. Even now, after he has become chairman of the chemistry department and has made outstanding progress in his profession as a research scientist and as director and consultant in corrosion research which has brought him recognition in *Who's Who in America,* there's still the expense of three children's education.

She made new doors conform to the original window

26

spaces they were replacing; saved doors and windows to be used later in other spots; and in adding on the dining room, she planned the three new walls to match the one exterior wall of Colonial type clapboard.

A double louvered door leads from the dining room into a huge living room at the front of the house. Another louvered door enters from living room into breakfast area of the kitchen. The living room was added the first year, but was only half its present size. It also has an old-fashioned looking pink brick fireplace that picks up the color in an original painting by William Lester, which hangs over the mantle. It was a gift from the artist and his wife, who are personal friends of the Hackermans.

House To Enjoy

Big windows with crisp white Priscilla organdy curtains, made by Mrs. Hackerman, enhance the inviting coziness of the living room and complement its Early American decor. This is "mama's room," and the children live up to prescribed rules when they want to enjoy its comfort — and, that is to "behave like grownups."

But the Hackerman home is a house that all the children and their friends love and enjoy, from the big screened play porch at back to the four cozy upstairs bedrooms that replaced the original two.

Up until this year, Mrs. Hackerman has been active in either Cub Scout or Girl Scout work, in addition to other civic and community activities. But the family got into a huddle and decided that "this is mama's year to do whatever she would like most to do." So, since she has always enjoyed writing, she has given up all other activities and is taking a journalism course at UT, and thoroughly enjoying it.

Even so, her mind is still making plans for her next remodeling project — a big glassed-in porch on top of the former garages.

The screened-in porch Lois described in her article soon thereafter became a glassed-in porch. Pat was in junior high school, and we needed a large enclosed space which was essentially indestructible and could be used by active teenagers summer and winter.

The Time Has Come

We had a virtually continuous parade of adolescents of both sexes in that house. Their hormones were jumping, making the teenagers themselves jump. Several of this crew had braces on their teeth. I spent part of my time making popcorn and baking cookies and mixing lemonade, and the other part cruising. I walked from kitchen to living room, through the dining room to the back porch seeing that all was well. Once I thought I would never get two of the children's braces unhooked! I finally did, and the youngsters returned to the party on the back porch as if nothing had happened.

Back to the jumping hormones. One delightful boy was Owen Revell. His parents were interior decorators and owned Revell Interiors. I remember one evening when his enthusiasm got the best of him and he jumped on the metal upholstered sofa swing, landing with both feet so as to bend the frame into a Murphy bed. As I watched this caper through the pass-through window from my kitchen vantage point, I was far from amused.

"Owen Revell," I said in my sternest voice, "you should know better. Your parents are in the furniture business. The party's over. Everybody go home."

After I saw them out, I returned to the kitchen and found Pat sobbing.

"Mother, how could you! They will never come back," she cried.

At the time, I hoped she was right, but I knew she wasn't. They were back many times.

I was happy that we had walled in this screened porch with windows. I had bunk beds built for slumber parties and lots of hanging pegboard space for baseball and ping pong equipment. After a few months, we added a television set and a secondhand pool table with folding legs. Pat and Steve learned to shoot pool here with their friends. Later I asked one of my student carpenters to make a ping pong table top from plywood. I painted it bright green and used white tape to rule off the lines.

The house actually grew around our family. As each child grew up, we truly needed space where a three-year-old could be penned up at the same time her eighteen-year-old sister could

28

Sharon Lane

have fifty sorority pledges going through their routines on the front law, using the pink brick patio Lois described in her article.

As Steve grew older, he needed space of his own, so I went upstairs, building a large area at the stairway landing, over the roof of the now-enclosed back porch. This became two rooms and a bath with a doorway between the bedrooms. Folding doors were installed, so it could be one big room for Steve. When Norm's father came to visit, the doors could be folded shut and Steve and Grandpa could have both privacy and togetherness.

Even before this addition, I realized that with so many youngsters in and out of the house, we needed a downstairs bathroom, other than Norm's and mine. So next to the enclosed back porch, I added a utility room with freezer, washer and dryer, commode and sink. The bathroom area could be closed off, and the utility part of the area served as a hallway to the backyard.

* * *

Whatever house I have lived in has always been full. Sometimes it's the children and their friends holding Brownie, Girl Scout or Cub Scout meetings. Sometimes it's just friends visiting. Pat especially seemed to be always surrounded by a gaggle of laughing, exuberant friends. Beginning in the early days at the University of Texas, Norm and I liked to entertain the chemistry faculty and their wives. Looking back, it seems everyone was young. Everyone had children, and everyone was working hard. Entertaining was easy — a casserole, a big green salad, hot biscuits, fruit, and lemon pie. Remember tuna casseroles? They were popular and simple to do, and they were the food of choice in the forties and fifties, at my parties, anyway.

I was proud of my lemon meringue pies, especially the crusts. I remember one Sunday afternoon baking three pies and leaving them on the kitchen table while I changed clothes. When I returned to the kitchen I found that Steve had climbed on the table, taken a spoon and eaten the meringue from every pie. I was dismayed. All my eggs were gone and in those days not a grocery store was open on Sunday. It was one of those events that had to be laughed off. Our guests ate "bald lemon meringue pies" and insisted they liked them that way.

29

The Time Has Come

Usually these get-togethers were food and conversation. Everyone sat or stood in the kitchen, laughing and exchanging stories about their work, their students, their children.

Sometimes we had bridge parties, maybe three tables of party bridge, with changes of partners every game. Bridge was popular then, and nearly everyone played.

These were planned parties, but other times Norm brought someone home for dinner — either a colleague at the university or some visitor from out of town. At Sharon Lane I had a large walk-in pantry with two wide and long top shelves. I kept there a stock of party food — things like smoked oysters, fancy canned fruits, crackers in tin boxes, cold soups, all foods that could supplement a meal or provide a snack for unexpected company.

This was before I had a recurring dream of the doorbell ringing and a bunch of dressed-up people standing on the doorstep, and I hadn't even been to the grocery store.

*   *   *

That sage called Anonymous once wrote that friendship is "two clocks keeping time." I have been fortunate to have a friend like that. Her name is Addie Mae. Long ago, when she was twenty and I was twenty-seven, both of us young mothers — I had two children, and she had three — entered a relationship, unspoken, to promote the good and happiness of one another.

One morning a slim, young black woman knocked on my front door, having heard that I was looking for a part-time maid.

"I'm Addie Mae Collins," said the woman at my door. "I've been working for Mrs. Ginsberg. The Ginsbergs are moving, and she heard that you might need help."

The year was 1946, nearly ten years before the U.S. Supreme Court knocked down the "separate but equal" concept for public schools, and twenty years before the Civil Rights Act. It was not only a different time, but a different world. It was unusual for a "person of color" (that's the way we talked then) to come to the front door and knock. I invited Addie Mae inside to have a cup of coffee and "talk things over" — the first of thousands of such discussions.

In those days, I was doing something I enjoyed and could do

30

at home, where I could both take care of the children and type theses and dissertations for Martha Ann Zivley. I could afford to have household help one-half day a week. Addie Mae said she enjoyed washing and ironing and loved children, so that was what she did one-half day a week the first year.

As time went on, we increased her time to three half-days a week. Gradually, by the time Steve was five or six, Addie Mae worked every morning. She washed and ironed while I typed and worked a number of part-time jobs — at the Well Log Service typing intricate tables; for Carl Hardin, filling in while his secretary was on vacation; for Mr. Meniere at the Texas Education Agency. All these jobs were in the mornings.

From the first, Addie Mae and I liked and trusted each other, but during the half-days she was at our house, we were both busy. We had little time for visiting. However, every day Addie Mae came to work for me, the first thing we did was sit down at the kitchen table and have coffee together. Addie Mae was my anchor and my friend. We had a relationship that would last a half-century, a kind of partnership in living that has sustained me through the years.

Addie Mae is gentle and loving, but she is also tough and strong.

While some people might enjoy looking at television or swimming or dancing, Addie Mae enjoys washing and ironing. She insists that she has always liked to do this. Even now, with all our children grown and gone, leaving us with little laundry to do, Norm and I have to be careful that Addie Mae doesn't snatch the shirts from our backs — just so she can wash them!

To an outsider it would seem Addie Mae and I were an unlikely pair. How, then, did we achieve this uncommon compatibility? We were both women. We both put our children at the center of our lives and shared our concerns and pride in them with each other. We had a lot of respect for each other. I thought she could do anything. She thought I could do anything. Actually, many times neither of us could do anything. One time we decided to make curtains. I thought she knew how, she thought I did. We just started making them, and somehow they looked fine.

Another time I decided to wallpaper the stairway at the

The Time Has Come

Sharon Lane house. I didn't know how, just started doing it — measuring and cutting, pasting and hanging. When it was done, Addie Mae and I admired it very much. It was cream-colored with a *fleur de lis* pattern. When my neighbor Marjorie Thomas came to look, she pointed out that the *fleur de lis* was upside down. Oh, well!

Besides working together on projects Addie Mae and I have always laughed a lot. And talked and talked, or worked in companionable silence. Addie Mae has always read books — as many as she has had time for. We talk about what we are reading and, after television, we have talked about programs we both see.

Addie Mae was so good with Steve and Pat. I felt confident in leaving them with her. So I took on teaching jobs at Nixon-Clay Business College and other temporary, part-time jobs.

Gradually, Addie Mae worked longer and longer hours at our house and became an important part of all our lives.

Addie Mae and I share the passion of womankind, a fierce dedication to our children, their well-being, their education. Addie Mae guarded my children from harm, grieved with them in their teenage disappointments, rejoiced in their triumphs, and I suspect even kept their confidences from me when she judged it would result in no harm.

She kept a careful check on our daughters' boyfriends, and, if Addie Mae found one lacking some attribute she believed necessary, he didn't last long.

Likewise I watched Addie Mae's children grow up. I was there with my handy Don Quixote sword to go charging toward the windmills when I felt someone or some institution was discriminating against Addie Mae or her children.

Addie Mae has one daughter, Ella, whom we called "Little Sister." When Little Sister married, Addie Mae and I planned the wedding around my kitchen table, sewed the veil, pulled out the punch bowl, and created a lovely affair in Addie Mae's garden.

Then one day Addie Mae called me, her voice trembling with despair and fright. "Little Sister is in labor," she said. "We are in the lobby at Brackenridge Hospital, and they won't take her upstairs because we don't have a hundred dollars."

Sharon Lane

"I'll be right there," I said. So I called Norm and told him I was going to write a hundred-dollar check and take it to the hospital.

"Do what you want to," he said.

When I arrived at Brackenridge, I found Addie Mae and a very frightened Little Sister. Her labor pains were coming one on top of the other. I don't remember ever being more angry. I marched into the social service office and said, "Can't you see that child is in labor and needs help?"

"This girl has known for nine months she was going to have a baby" said the social worker. "She could have been saving her money all that time . . ."

Another windmill to fight appeared at Scarbrough's Department Store, then at Sixth and Congress in downtown Austin.

Every fall I took Steve to Scarbrough's to buy his school shoes. I also took Addie Mae's two boys for shoes. I walked into Scarbrough's with three little boys — two black and one white — and sat down in the shoe department. Mr. Barton, who had waited on me many times before, seemed uneasy.

"What can I do for you?" he asked.

"I want shoes for these boys."

"I'm sorry, Mrs. Hackerman. I'm not allowed to wait on colored people."

"Mr. Barton," I said, "will you please go upstairs to the office and tell the manager that if I can't buy shoes for these boys, I won't buy anything in this store ever again?"

Mr. Barton scooted off to some higher place, returning after a while to say, "I'm sorry about offending you, but you'll have to go to the basement. Someone will wait on you there."

I fear we sometimes forget the hurt that society and its rules inflicted in those days.

While I was working with Girl Scouts and Brownies, I invited Scout leaders from all over Austin to Sharon Lane for coffee. One of the leaders from the East Austin troops came.

After the meeting was over, a neighbor came to my house and asked, "Was that a colored lady you had as a visitor?"

"Yes," I answered.

"We don't do that in Tarrytown," she said.

Chapter 6

Alice

n the 1940s, young women in Austin were protected from the snares of the big city. At the University of Texas, they lived in dormitories — either University-owned or operated by the Masonic Order (Scottish Rite Dormitory) or the Methodist Church (Kirby Hall). Women students came and went under strict curfews, signing out at their dormitories' main desk even to go to the library, and certainly to go on a date. At 10:55 P.M., every dormitory entrance was crowded with young couples kissing and literally being torn apart by blinking lights, signaling that the girls must go inside. Those who didn't live in the dormitories lived in residences called "approved housing." The dean of women was responsible for assuring that this housing was safe, clean and supervised. Her name was Dorothy Gebauer.

This kind of surveillance extended throughout the community. Nixon-Clay Business College operated a thriving day and night school in downtown Austin. The college had an excellent reputation for turning out skilled typists and stenographers, bookkeepers, and office managers. Nixon-Clay attracted high school graduates from within a 150-mile radius of Austin, not just because of its excellent instruction, but because state government offices offered opportunities for employment in Austin to competent typists and office workers.

I was always on the lookout for part-time jobs to supplement Norm's assistant professor salary. Besides, I liked to work at a

Alice

variety of jobs, enjoying the learning that always accompanied different work experiences.

Nixon-Clay had been started by two men — Mr. Nixon and Mr. Clay. When I went down to apply for a night teaching job, Mr. Clay's widow owned the school. She hired me. I thought Mrs. Clay showed a great deal of personal interest in the students. She was careful to find them good places to stay, either in boarding-houses, which were still plentiful in those days, or in Austin homes. She usually tried to find young couples with children who would give girls room and board in exchange for helping with the children and doing light housework.

I thought this was a good service, both for Nixon-Clay students and for their families. Our friends, Jack and Evelyn Myers, had four daughters and always had a girl from Nixon-Clay to help Evelyn with the children.

I taught in the night school for about six months while I was pregnant with Steve. After we moved to Sharon Lane, Steve was born and I forgot all about Nixon-Clay. Several years passed by and one day Mrs. Clay called me. She said the daytime typing and shorthand teacher had become ill and had to have an operation. Mrs. Clay asked if I would substitute for her.

This was how I met Alice. Just out of high school, Alice was from a Central Texas town and an outstanding student. She enjoyed being the fastest typist in the class. She was an attractive, slim, dark-haired girl, friendly and outgoing. After completing the Nixon-Clay courses, Alice easily got a job as a bookkeeper in the office of a local business.

The regular typing-shorthand teacher recuperated from her surgery and returned to work, and I went on my merry way. By that time, I had another interesting part-time job which allowed me to take the children along. I saw an advertisement in the *Austin American* for a "shopper." This appealed to me. I liked to shop, especially if it wouldn't cost me any money. A drug store chain in town had a line of products, its own brand. The chain was pushing these products, but feared their salespersons weren't being aggressive enough in selling them. They hired me to go from store to store, asking for "toothpaste" or "soap." In those days, drugstore shelves were not open to the shopper; a

35

person had to ask a clerk for the product. My assignment was to keep a record of which clerks encouraged me to buy the store product. I was to buy the merchandise, then turn it in for a refund at the end of the week. I was paid fifty cents an hour and ten cents a mile for use of my car.

Several months after I had left Nixon-Clay, Steve and I were downtown when we met John Clemens, a Nixon-Clay teacher. I had promised Steve, then about four years old, a toy from Woolworth's and we were nearing the store. Steve was less than enthusiastic about my stopping to talk with Mr. Clemens. Steve kept tugging on my hand, trying to pull me along, and jumping up and down. But Mr. Clemens had some interesting, disturbing news.

"Have you heard about Alice?" he asked.

"No, I haven't seen her since I left the college."

"She's in deep trouble," he said.

"For heaven's sake . . . what did she do?" I asked. I couldn't believe Alice would have a problem at work. She was dependable and confident in her skills. My only thought was perhaps an error in her accounts.

"She's in trouble . . . trouble, you know," Mr. Clemens answered.

"No, I don't know. What's wrong with Alice?"

"She's going to have a baby, and she's about to be put out of her boardinghouse," Mr. Clemens said.

"Are you going to do anything about it?" I asked him.

"I can't do anything," he answered. "I'm married."

Steve and I went on to Woolworth's, where I bought him a toy car. When we returned to our car, a policeman was writing a parking ticket. I told him I had just had some worrisome news, so he gave me a warning. I hope the policeman didn't hear Steve say in a loud voice, "Mom, he's got *funny* teeth."

I went directly to Nixon-Clay and into Mrs. Clay's office. I told her what Mr. Clemens had said and asked her, "What can we do?"

I'll never forget her answer, "Nothing: She made her bed; now she can lie in it."

"I want to get in touch with her," I told Mrs. Clay. "Do you have her address?"

Alice

The next day I called Alice and asked her to lunch at the Hitching Post, for years a popular restaurant on Lamar Boulevard, just north of the Colorado River. Alice had lost her job, and her landlady had asked her to move.

I picked Alice up, and we went to the Hitching Post. We ordered, then I asked Alice, "Why don't you tell me what is wrong? Mr. Clemens said you are in trouble."

That question broke open the gates. Crying and clutching my hands, Alice told me she was three months pregnant, that the father of the baby had told his parents that they were going to be married, and they said, "over our dead bodies," or words to that effect. The boy who fathered the baby was in the university and the son of a prominent contractor and builder, and the family was well known.

"Last night and the night before, I walked down to the Congress Avenue Bridge, planning to jump into the river and kill myself. Oh, Mrs. Hackerman, I just couldn't do it. I don't know what to do."

"Does your mother know?" I asked her.

"No, I can't tell her."

"Well," I said. "I'll take you to your boardinghouse. You go in, pack up your stuff, and I'll come back for you in about an hour. We'll think of something to do."

When I got home to Sharon Lane, I called Norm and asked him if it was all right for Alice to stay with us a few days.

"Anything you do is all right with me," he answered, "but just keep her out of sight."

I fixed up the other half of our attached garage as a room for Alice, moving a roll-away bed into the space and a dresser, and hanging curtains to hide the washer and dryer. I used the other half of the garage as my typing room. By this time I was typing chemistry theses for Martha Ann Zivley's Typing Service.

I told Alice she must tell her parents what was happening, but I wanted to do it with as little trauma as possible for both them and Alice. However, I could not assume responsibility for her without their consent.

"We need to get in touch with your parents," I told her. "You need to be at home with them."

37

The Time Has Come

"Oh no," she said. "That's impossible. My father is running for public office and my little sister is going through sorority rush at the university. This will ruin everything."

"Well, I have to call them," I said.

"Be very careful what you say," she begged. "Everybody is on the party line."

I promised I wouldn't say anything on the telephone to give away the situation. I spoke with Alice's mother and asked her if she could come down to Austin on the bus, indicating that I wanted to talk with her about Alice going with us on a trip during the summer to help with the children.

The following Sunday, Alice's mother did come to Austin. Norm took Pat and Steve to San Antonio to the zoo, so only Alice and I would be at the house.

I met her mother at the bus station, and then drove up Congress Avenue. I told her right away that Alice was pregnant and needed our help. She fainted as we drove through the Capitol grounds. I shook her awake, told her we were going to my house and talk it over with Alice.

I made some coffee for us and I left Alice alone with her mother in the house, and took my cup of coffee and book to a swing in a grove of trees in the yard and read while they talked. Two hours later, I went into the house.

"Can *you* take care of her?" asked Alice's mother.

"She can stay here for a while," I told her, "but we can't be responsible for her medical care."

I suggested a Methodist home in San Antonio that I had heard was a safe haven for unwed expectant mothers.

"Oh, no," said Alice's mother. "We have so many friends in San Antonio. Alice would surely run into some of them."

We agreed that Alice would stay with us for three or four months, that I would put her under the medical care of Dr. Maribel Loving, a woman obstetrician I knew. Alice was a careful and competent typist, so I got extra work from Mrs. Zivley for her. With this money, she could buy incidentals and maternity clothes.

It was summertime. We did not go away that summer. Every other Sunday, I took my children and Alice to Georgetown, where Alice met her parents at Georgetown Park. They visited and picnicked and tried to sort out the future. I would pack a picnic lunch for Pat and Steve and me and we would find a private table away from Alice's family so they could have privacy.

The parents needed a cover story. Where was Alice when their friends asked? Earlier, the mother had told people that Alice was going away to Baltimore for the summer with us, and the parents needed some letters from Alice from Baltimore. Alice wrote her parents; she put the letters in an addressed and stamped envelope, and I sent them in another envelope to my friend Rita Johns in Baltimore. Rita then mailed Alice's letters from Baltimore to her hometown, and the nosy postmaster could see the Baltimore postmark.

Fall was coming on. It was nearly time for Alice's sister to go to her rush parties, and the political campaigning was in full tilt. Dr. Loving recommended a maternity home in Kansas City. Alice wanted to keep the baby, but her parents were adamant, "That's out of the question."

I took Alice on the MKT passenger train to Kansas City, promising her mother, "If it's not the kind of place I'd be willing to leave my own child, I'll bring her home."

I took her to the home, and as the taxi let us out on the broad steps, I had an awful feeling of sadness that this child would be all alone to deliver her first child. I almost said, "I'll stay," but of course, that was ridiculous. I had my own children to get back to. After she and I talked with the director, a pleasant, kindly woman, I hugged Alice goodbye and left. Then I walked down the circular driveway and sat on the bench by the bus stop and cried.

Alice stayed in Kansas City, had her baby, gave the little girl away for adoption, and came back to Austin and us. She stayed for just a month or so in her little room in the garage. At night, I could hear her sobbing, crying for the lost baby and what she perceived as a lost love. Sometimes I slipped out of bed and went into her room, sat by her bed and silently held her hand. There was nothing I could say. I could only cry with her. Norm gave her a temporary job in his office so she could earn a little before she went home.

The Time Has Come

After her father's election — I don't remember if he won or lost — Alice went home. I told her goodbye at the bus station.

"Alice, you will pull your life together," I told her. "I'll think about you often, but there's no need to keep in contact. Perhaps it would be better if you forget all about this time in your life."

I had done nothing extraordinary for Alice, only what I could in that time and circumstance. My continuing belief is that we do for others as much as we can, and somehow this love and caring will be distributed further. We repay the good things others do for us, but not necessarily to the people whom we owe. That's the way love is disseminated. We can't outgive the Lord; we have to keep paying back.

Two years after I put Alice on the bus, she called one day and said she would like to come see me.

She was radiant, doing fine. She had a job in Central Texas and she was going to be married.

"Should I tell him?" she asked.

"I can't make that decision for you," I answered. "I know what I would do, but I won't even tell you what that would be. Ask God to help you make the right decision. I wish you joy and happiness in whatever you do."

We embraced and she was gone. I never heard from her again.

Chapter 7

No Homogenized Degrees

To a person who loves books and learning, living around or on university campuses is as intoxicating as living in a casino would be to a gambler. As soon as the children were in school, I began taking or auditing courses at the University of Texas. It never entered my head to pursue a degree; my interests were too eclectic. Actually, the courses I chose were the ones I thought at the time I needed for day-to-day life, to gain the skills and know-how for either some project I wanted to do, like home design, or for some subject I wanted to explore, like the American novel.

When I was building and decorating houses, I took design courses. When I wanted to draw and paint, I took art classes. When I wanted to write about my projects, I took feature writing in the Journalism School.

Before signing up for a class to audit, I made a point to check in with the dean or chairman of a college or department. I wanted to be sure my presence wouldn't be distracting to the teacher or the other students. By doing this, I became acquainted with many university greats — for example, Dr. DeWitt Reddick in journalism and Dr. Margaret Eppright in home economics. Dr. Reddick was one of those rare people who could have taught anything, just because he had that quality of believing in every individual and making that person, in turn, believe in himself. Dr. Eppright, one of the most quotable of women, is still known around the campus for her good-natured feminism. Once, when pressed with too many duties, too little time, with the responsi-

41

bilities of her career as well as running a home, she said, "What I need is a wife."

It was in an interior design class on furniture that I met Wayne Bell, a fellow student, who later was commissioned by Miss Ima Hogg to restore the historical dwellings at Winedale, the property near Roundtop which Miss Hogg donated to the University of Texas. Now Winedale is the home of musical concerts and the summer Shakespeare Festival.

Wayne also assisted Miss Hogg in collecting the period furniture which now resides in the house named Bayou Bend, which Miss Hogg bequeathed to the Houston Museum of Fine Arts.

I took the design course after Pat married. She was an interior design major and left a collection of design equipment — templates, and who knows what else — when she moved to California. What was I to do but find some use for them?

Wayne Bell was a friend of Cad and Frances Williams, and a frequent visitor at their home. They were our next door neighbors on Sharon Lane. After our class together, Wayne and I often talked and compared notes on various of my building projects. I remember especially receiving some advice from him on building a lily pond. Wayne was visiting the Williamses one afternoon about cocktail time and the three of them were sitting on the Williamses' side porch, chatting happily, ice clinking in their glasses. At the same time, some distance away, two small children and one adult were also happily chattering and patting wet concrete into the bottom of a fish pond the adult had finished building. Bailey, the Williamses' little boy, Katy, my little girl, and I talked back and forth with the other group as we worked. We were trying to finish before dark. Much advice was shouted to us on how to hurry along and finish. The shouters were having a grand old time! Their advice was worthless.

I also took Richard King's feature-writing course. One of his requirements was that each student get ten rejection slips from magazine editors for proposals for articles. Of course, he would have preferred that we receive acceptance letters, but he was a realist, wanting to spark ideas and enough gumption to try them out on editors. Also, I believe he wanted us to learn to take rejection without giving up. It's disheartening to collect just *one* rejection slip.

I sent some greeting-card poems and ideas to Hallmark Cards. A Hallmark editor wrote he was interested in my work and asked how many greeting card ideas I could generate. He asked if I would like to work out some kind of contract. I didn't follow through on this. I knew I could do what I set out to do — learn how to do it. It was not necessary to make a career of greeting cards, but only to know I could if I had to!

Norm encouraged me in my smorgasbord approach to learning, remarking that I had taken enough courses for a homogenized degree; but that no university gives that! The degree part never enticed me, but the knowledge did. There was also *so* much to learn, so much information just waiting for me to grab it, to satisfy my appetite for knowing how, when, where, what, who, why.

The university was my candy store — offering sweet little tidbits from the music performances, a touch of rich fudge from the Department of Drama presentations, the opportunity to chew on political issues discussed by visiting speakers at the Texas Union, and small delicacies of ancient food for thought at an archaeological lecture. Last, but not least, the university offered a taste of divinity as Dean William Doty of the School of Fine Arts played heavenly music on the university organ at a Sunday afternoon concert.

As Jackie Gleason would say, "How sweet it was!"

*   *   *

The decade of the forties cradled halcyon days between Staten Island and Blacksburg for the first five years, and then Austin, Texas, for the last five. During the Staten Island–Blacksburg period, Norm was gone eighteen months, working on the atom bomb. Since the project was top secret, I didn't know what he was doing in New York until 1945. The bomb was dropped on Hiroshima after we came to Austin.

The last five years of the forties saw us in Austin, Norm happy at the university, and I happy with Pat and a new baby boy.

The Time Has Come

We welcomed the fifties with new Texas friends in our house on Sharon Lane.

I took Steve and Pat upstairs to bed as our guests were gathered around the piano in the kitchen singing "Auld Lang Syne." The notes floated up the stairway, and I thought, as I tucked the children in, that my world was perfect. I was young and had no hint of what the next decade would hold.

Chapter 8

The Quintessential Volunteer

My mother died when I was two years old. My only memory of her is a vivid scene forever etched in my consciousness. It is of a beautiful sleeping woman lying in a box in the parlor of my grandmother's house in Baltimore. It was my mother, dressed in a soft, white dress. Someone lifted me to see her . . . that's all I remember. I know I asked, "Where is Mama?"

My grandmother told me that she had gone to heaven. In later years, my grandmother also told me that I often climbed up onto a chair by the table where the telephone stood, asking to talk to Mama in heaven.

I don't remember this at all, but, strangely, I remember my grandmother's early telephone number — Homewood 4965J!

After I was two years old, I never had a mother, so in Austin, Texas, when my own children were growing up, I did my mothering by trial and error. Lacking a role model, I gave it my best.

In the fall of 1950, Pat was seven years old — old enough to join a Girl Scout troop as a Brownie. I went one day to Girl Scout headquarters and said to the receptionist, "My name is Gene Hackerman. I would like to be a Brownie leader. Can you give me some information?"

The young woman scurried into Opal Clifton's office. Opal Clifton was executive director of the Girl Scout organization in Central Texas.

"Lock the door," said Mrs. Clifton, coming out to meet me.

45

The Time Has Come

Thus began both a warm friendship with Opal and years of delightful companionship with my own daughters and girls their age.

"I'm a Brownie leader," I told Norm that evening.

"Hell, you've always been a Brownie!" he replied. He was right.

*　　*　　*

New Brownie leaders were required to take a training course before the Girl Scout organization would turn us loose on other people's children. Another of the new leaders who was in my training group was Marye Benjamin, whom we called Chub. An irrepressible humor bubbled inside this very bright woman.

Since her husband had their car every day, she rode with me to our training sessions, back and forth to Radio House at the University of Texas, where she was a writer. Every day we learned singing, dancing, jumping up and down, and how to become a genuine Brownie. We learned how to:

> Jump down, turn around, pick a bale of cotton;
> Jump down, turn around, pick a bale a day.

This was an action song, and my actions were fairly good, but I'm not a singer. On the last day of training, I drove Chub back to Radio House and said goodbye. Her final words to me were, "I hate to think of a whole generation of little girls learning to sing off-key."

At Brownie Leader Training, I learned recipes for cookouts, which I have adapted to cook-ins. One of my family's favorites, then and now, is Farmer's Delight.

For a cookout, the chef needs a metal coffee can, a pound of hamburger, one chopped onion, one can vegetable soup (no water added, please) and one can kidney beans. Mix the ingredients, pour them into the coffee can, and seal the can with aluminum foil. Place the can under the coals of an open fire, and sit back and let it cook. When everyone is hungry, dig out the coffee can and serve. There's no set time for cooking. If the meat is too pink, roll the whole thing in the coals again.

My first Brownie troop was organized on November 3, 1950. Sixteen little girls, seven-year-old second-graders, met at my house every week. We elected officers, including a secretary to record the activities of each meeting. The minutes survive, with these one-sentence entries: "We practiced our service." "We sang songs." "We made ashtrays out of old records." "We talked about going on a hike. Then we made candy." "We went to the Museum [Texas Memorial Museum]. We picked up fossils on Shoal Creek." "We made moth ball dolls." [With wire, the girls strung moth balls into the shape of a doll. These gadgets could be hung in closets to repel moths.]

Perhaps my favorite of the entries in the minutes of the Brownie meetings that first year is this springtime account: "We went to the seed house. We went to the park and got some dirt to plant our zinnias. We planted the seeds in cigar boxes. Some grew, but most didn't."

Now, four decades later, I still run into some of these Brownies, all grown up, and mothers now themselves, some even grandmothers, and they stop and speak: "Oh, Mrs. Hackerman, do you remember me? I was in your Brownies." Even as I write, a member of Katy's group is sending out letters to organize a reunion of Brownies for Katy's years.

Among my happiest memories of those years are recollections of the children I was fortunate enough to get to know through their Brownie and Girl Scout years. I still hold them in my heart.

Just in case any reader wants to be a Brownie leader, I advise you to hold on to the thought. Try it. You may like it. I found my first year as a Brownie leader rewarding. I must admit to the days when I wondered if I could get away with slipping off to the movies and forgetting the whole thing. But most days, I would have turned down large amounts of money if someone had tried to bribe me to give up my Brownies. Not having the Brownies would have meant losing the company of those curious, energetic, occasionally quarrelsome little girls, as well as an occasional assistant leader, and something of myself, too, and what I consider the best of myself — having fun and teaching the little, enthusiastic people. Women who spend their time working in the Brownie and Girl Scout programs get more out of it than the children do, I truly believe. It makes one's life more worthwhile in many ways.

I called myself the Old Brown Owl, and she is still hooting just as loudly as ever, despite the gray feathers in her topknot. Opal Clifton asked me to put down some of the activities we did for a little training manual for Brownie leaders. We called this booklet "The Old Owl Hoots" or "How to Be a Brownie Leader in 10 Easy Lessons."

One page sums up my delight in working with the little girls:

> And then, of course, there are the times when thirteen little girls sing sweetly the Brownie song, say their Promise in all seriousness and conduct a meeting in a very adult way;
>
> when thirteen grimy little girls chop up onions, scurry around for firewood, apply Band-Aids to each other for minor scratches, and obviously enjoy a cookout;
>
> when thirteen quiet and industrious little girls labor over painting Christmas presents for their mothers;
>
> when starry-eyed little girls exclaim after a trip to ride on the glass-bottomed boats at San Marcos, "This was the best trip, ever!"
>
> when really impressed little girls tip-toe softly around the library and sign up for library cards;
>
> when happy little girls laugh and joke about their silly puppets;
>
> when mothers call the leader to say they think our troop is a fine one;
>
> and when the Old Brown Owl realizes how fortunate she is to have so many nice little girls in her troop.

One year we had a handicapped child in our troop who had to walk on crutches. Jack Mason, one of the fathers who annually drove us for Christmas carol singing, carried her from his car to each front porch so she could participate fully. Brownie parents helped often and consistently.

*   *   *

All together, I spent fourteen years in scouting — seven years with Pat in Brownies and Girl Scouts, two years with Steve in Cub Scouts, three years with Sally in Brownies and two years with Katy.

The Quintessential Volunteer

During these Brownie sessions, I had no one to leave Steve with, so I took him along on the Girl Scout outings. He complained constantly about being the only boy. I promised him that as soon as he was old enough, he would be a Cub Scout. And so he was. And guess who was the den mother!

Boys cannot become Cub Scouts until they are eight, but when Steve was seven, he *thought* he was a Scout. We organized a little den which we called the Scrub Scouts. Of course, this group had nothing to do with official scouting, but it gave Steve the outlet he had been waiting for. The Scrub Scout members were Steve's friends from school.

I took Steve and his friends for outdoor activities, usually centered at Westenfield Park. The boys did such activities as developing a balance-beam act and conducting innumerable races. Steve always liked to run, and even at seven, he was unconsciously training for the track he ran throughout his high school years.

From the time he was six, he would run down our 150- foot driveway at Sharon Lane. "Time me, Mama, time me," he yelled. I actually bought a stopwatch, and every time he made that round trip between house and street, I'd stand on the porch and time him. He was so good about bringing the empty garbage containers back from the street because this chore gave him another reason for running his course.

Another favorite activity of the boys was climbing on the jungle gym. They called it the "jingle jam," and Steve calls it that to this day.

While Steve was in Cub Scouts at Casis, we den mothers produced the Casis School Circus, known as the "Tingling Mothers Circus." The boys and their mothers had a splendid time doing this. I wrote the script in verse and narrated the show, which delighted the little boys. We had a two-headed man (two little boys' heads coming out of a large sweatshirt that encased their bodies), clowns and acrobats, including daring young men on high-wire. The high wire was actually not so high. Well, it was four inches off the floor, a two-by-four laid across the stage. And let us not forget the tattooed man (who was literally covered with grotesque "tattoos" executed with my eyebrow pencil). The lion's mane was a new fluffy string mop.

The Time Has Come

The lion himself was two boys — one at the back, and the other at the front of the costume.

For the high wire act, the boys wore tights and frilly tutus while balancing themselves with pink ruffled parasols made by the same mother. The tutus were designed and made by one of the mothers who had no girls. She said, "This may be my only chance to sew something frilly."

The sideshow acts included a strong man, the tattooed man, the dog-faced boy, the bearded lady, the snake charmer, the sword swallower, and, of course, the two-headed man.

The circus required coordination among five dens — five den mothers and forty frisky little boys.

This was just one example of the fun we had. The boys worked up another program, "Famous Moments in History," in which they acted out such sayings as "Don't shoot until you see the whites of their eyes." For this one, they rigged up a mask with eyes that were all white. Pocahontas was there with her black braids and Sir Walter Raleigh with his ever-ready cloak to put across mud puddles for the ladies to walk on. And let me not forget Miles Standish, Priscilla and John Alden, and Priscilla's great moment, "Speak for yourself, John."

When I became a Brownie leader and when I was appointed or elected to various jobs with the University Ladies Club, I believed these to be extensions of homemaking — providing creative activities for my children and sharing in the university life of my husband. At that time, I had no philosophy of volunteerism.

In some quarters, volunteerism had a bad name. I remember hearing one woman say, "Volunteers are worth what they get paid." She thought her remark was terribly funny.

Others have been more kind. J. W. Edgar, long-time Texas commissioner of education, once said he wouldn't work for a school that had no Parent-Teacher Association. Irby Carruth, superintendent of the Austin Independent School District while my children were in school, was the keynote speaker at the State Convention of Parents and Teachers one year. He began his speech, "What are you doing here? Why aren't you home with your children?" Then he addressed the urgent need for strong parent involvement in the schools. "Only through parents interested enough to take an active part in Parent-Teacher Associations can great school systems be built," he said.

A friend once asked me, "Gene, do you ever say 'No' to any request for your time?" I found this a strange question. Of course I do. My interests and energies have always been focused on children, music and art, issues related to cancer, and educational-related activities.

The area which I have consistently rejected for myself is politics. When Adele Black retired from the Austin Independent School District Board of Trustees, she suggested to me that I run for the place she was vacating. I realized the large amount of time such a position would take, and I knew also that I was not emotionally equipped for politics. In many ways, I know I am strong, but I don't believe I could stand for my family to be subjected to criticisms of some action I might take as a member of a public board. In a political position, controversy cannot be avoided, and enemies are made. Running for office is the only volunteer area which I have avoided.

Volunteer work in Austin and Houston has provided me with opportunities for growth and learning that I may not have had in a more focused job. My joy in doing community service may well be living out one of my grandmother's truisms: "If you don't have what you want, you'd better want what you have." I wanted what I had in volunteer work, satisfaction in doing a job well; participation with my children in their activities; helping in the community; and supporting Norm by supporting his university.

Two talents I recognized in myself are for organization and for the more creative activities — writing verse, drawing cartoons, thinking up games and other exhilarating ways to entertain and stimulate children, and finding ways the impossible can be done. I don't believe in "can't," and my children grew up on "The Little Engine That Could."

In 1968, after some seventeen years of intensive volunteering, I was asked to participate in a television program produced at KLRN-TV for national telecast. It took us three hours, with breaks for coffee, to tape an hour show. The program was entitled, "How To Be Human." The other participants were two distinguished University of Texas professors, Dr. Fillmore Sanford, a psychologist, and Dr. Charles Bonjean, a sociologist. The moderator was Pat Green. The professors, both of national stature, spoke of the necessity to be involved in state, national and even international issues. They talked about joining the Peace Corps, feeding people in other countries, and other far-away projects. As they talked, I realized that what I had to say was rather provincial and maybe Pollyannaish. I did not apologize, but suggested that activities such as working with the children in your neighborhood, helping out when someone's house across town burns to the ground, or organizing a Symphony League in your city to promote music for all are provincial, but they are so in the best sense of the word. Most of us can't climb Mt. Everest, or be the first woman to walk on the moon, but all of us can make the place we live and the neighborhood around us better — more attractive, safer, cleaner, more cooperative.

Another important aspect to volunteer work is that the activities one participates in come in phases, reflecting the various passages of one's life. For example, I wouldn't volunteer to be a Brownie leader now that I am in my seventies. Being a Brownie leader takes physical attributes I no longer have. I cannot "jump down, turn around, pick a bale of cotton" — and I don't want to! Every person's mental, physical and emotional energies and capabilities change, and so should her contributions to the community.

Sometimes, now, when I am invited to spend time on some worthwhile project, I may decline, but say, "I'll send a contribution."

Even organizations have their passages, especially Parent-Teacher Associations. The mothers and fathers of kindergarteners and first graders are much more excited about becoming involved in school activities than are the parents of high school students. High school PTAs, thus, are squeezed in double binds: the needs of high schools for enrichment money are always large and the energy of the parent members is usually at low ebb. Most have been active in PTA for at least ten years. They have already baked the cakes, sold the tickets, decorated the booths, painted scary faces on children, mustarded the hot dogs, and come home exhausted year after year from "the carnival."

This was where we were in 1958, when I was chairman of the

The Quintessential Volunteer

Publicity Committee of the Austin High School PTA and came up with the idea of a "Stay Home Carnival." The executive committee met early in the summer and made a "blueprint" of the year's programs. (For years I had been working with blueprints building our house at Sharon Lane, thus the blueprint idea.) We listed a program, "You are Sidewalk Superintendents," another on "Your Project is at the Half-Way Point," and another on questions about curriculum. The blueprint program, however, was strangely silent about the big money raiser — the PTA Carnival. Only a hint that something different was in the offing came in Sue Brandt McBee's column, "Hereabouts," in the *Austin American-Statesman:* "Yet a big secret to most members of the STEPHEN F. AUSTIN PTA are plans for the year's program being *blueprinted* by some of its ingenious officers . . . the CHARLES HERRINGS . . . THE NORMAN HACKERMANS . . . and the HOMER GARRISONS."

I received more publicity than I bargained for when I took a copy of the blueprint program by the newspaper office and left it for the editor, Charles E. Green. I wanted him to see what a good job Windy Winn had done in designing the sketches for the programs.

A staff member left the editor the following memo: "A most attractive lady brought this most attractive PTA Austin High Yearbook by for you to see. She was tall, with grey-blue eyes, and slightly curly hair that looked natural in its wave. I guess she was Mrs. Norman Hackerman, as she said to tell you the publicity chairman came by."

And this is what CEG wrote in his column, run along with the memo: "It must have been, for your description fits her to a T. She has a daughter, Patricia, in high school, a younger son, Steve, a daughter, Sally, in kindergarten, and a beautiful baby. Her husband, Dr. Norman Hackerman, is a research scientist and, I think, head man in the UT Chemistry Department. They loved her at Casis because she always seemed to have time to do the many things required of volunteer workers."

As school and the PTA program activities of the year got under way, the carnival committee kept its big surprise under wraps. The surprise: No carnival. But how about money for the

PTA's budget, for all the extras the PTA always did for the school?

The secret was out December 5 in a headline in the *Austin Maroon*, the school newspaper: "Families to Stay Home for 'Marooned' Carnival."

It was an idea that everyone endorsed. But the executive committee had the job of making it work. We had to keep our eye on the goal — to make enough money to take care of the PTA's responsibilities to the school, to fulfill the commitments we had made. And we had to make it worthwhile for patrons of the school to give money to stay home. Door prizes, donated by Austin merchants and friends of Austin High School, was the answer. We rounded up support from media personalities like Cactus Pryor and Bill Quay to award the door prizes. And we received the cooperation of the management of KTBC-TV and Radio for these gentlemen to use their air time to award prizes.

Texas used to have stout laws against lotteries, so we couldn't sell chances for the door prizes. That would have constituted a lottery. I talked with Senator Charles Herring, an eminent lawyer, and the attorney general of Texas, Will Wilson, about the problem. They agreed that we couldn't sell chances and suggested that we ask for cash contributions. The following flyer (next two pages) was sent home with every student at Austin High.

We were also committed to keeping our Stay-At-Home Carnival as hassle-free as possible for the school administrators and teachers. We wrote a script for the public address system at the school and prepared instructions for the home room teachers to follow in handling the money donated.

It worked! The Marooned Carnival received good publicity marks throughout the state — including the *Dallas Morning News*. In the local newspaper, Lorraine Barnes wrote:

> Fortunately, the Austin High PTA people have thought of a solution to this wayward custom (PTA carnivals) and at only a fraction of the cost of kicking around a night club all night. They're staging a "Marooned Carnival" Thursday night, and the only way of going to it is to stay home. People who rush out somewhere, probably from force of habit, aren't playing it cricket.

54

The Quintessential Volunteer

As the PTA sees it, Austin High families will gladly donate to a worthy cause — in this case the PTA — for the privilege of staying home from a school carnival. Austin merchants, many of whom have children in the school and would like an evening with their shoes off — are contributing some 35 valuable prizes as inducements to staying home.

This is a noble experiment and we only wish somebody had thought of it a few years back when it would have done us, an Austin High PTA alum, the most good. If it succeeds, who knows? A grateful nation might raise a monument to the Austin Idea.

We commend the sponsors of this unique enterprise in the glowingest terms of which we are capable. Familial integration, it's here, and in the spirit of the movement we hope you give it a try yourselves some night, just sitting quietly in a left-wing, right-wing arm chair and letting your thoughts dwell where they may — on a book, a newspaper, radio, television or the Christmas party that'll drag you out next.

The executive committee, the same people who had worried they wouldn't collect enough money to pay the $600 the PTA owed for fans for the school, happily counted $2,100. It was a great victory for the PTA and for all parents who like to stay home.

I personally enjoyed the carnival, although it was an all-consuming project for several months. My colleagues on the committee, and later the Seventh District Conference of Parents and Teachers, gave me credit for a job well done. But the most extravagant praise appeared in Sue McBee's column, "Hereabouts," Sunday, December 14, 1958:

> In all the terrific publicity about Austin High School's laborless "Marooned Carnival" . . . which, at this writing, had already brought in more than $2,000 to the PTA coffers . . . did the person who, to our personal knowledge, labored endless hours for several months on the project ever get suitable recognition?
>
> She is GENE (Mrs. Norman) HACKERMAN . . . who manages to be beautiful, brainy, motherly, artistic, and civic all at the same time.

The Time Has Come

STAY HOME   Your PTA URGES you to   STAY HOME !

THE MAROONED CARNIVAL

presents

A RARE TREAT.

A lovely, lazy evening at home with your family

WE JUST GOTTA HAVE A SUCCESSFUL FUND-RAISING

Please fill in the coupon below, with your figures, and send your money in the enclosed envelope.

Then

Stay

Home!

Read your newspaper.   Listen to KTBC-TV and radio.   Cactus Pryor and Bill Quay will award the wonderful door prizes on their shows, December 11.

Every Austin High family (student and faculty) is eligible to win . . .

| silver | blankets | down pillows | free dinners | records |
| bowling tickets | gift certificates | happy surprises | | |

YOU HAVE TO BE HOME TO WIN

BUT

YOU WON'T HAVE TO:

Beg donations	then	Try to sell them
Decorate a stand	then	Tear it down
Bake a cake	then	Buy it back
Pay a sitter	then	Take her home
Sell cold drinks	then	Go home thirsty
Serve hot dogs	then	Eat them cold
Stock a booth	then	Peddle your wares
Buy a white elephant	then	Try to hide it.

ALL YOU'RE ASKED TO DO IS SEND MONEY

BEFORE Wednesday, December 10, send money

IN envelope

BY child

TO school

We're still in the red $600 for fans
Get us back in the black!

THIS COUPON ENTITLES: Mr. and Mrs. _____

PHONE: _____ ADDRESS _____

To enjoy the Austin High PTA Carnival Marooned at home.

Valuable Coupon

TIME SAVED	WE VALUE AT	$_____
EVENING AT HOME	WE VALUE AT	$_____
ENERGY CONSERVED	WE VALUE AT	$_____
PURCHASES NOT MADE	WE VALUE AT	$_____
TOTAL CONTRIBUTION TO MAROONED CARNIVAL		$_____

It's Deductible!

P.S.

Make checks to Austin High P?

The Quintessential Volunteer

Austin High Marooned Carnival

MAROONED......
    With the people you love most
    At the place you like best.

MAROONED CARNIVAL CONTRIBUTION

Name_____

Address_____

Telephone Number_____

Chapter 9

Pat, Miracle Child

W hen Pat was in the second grade, Mrs. T. H. Williams, the mother of Knox Williams, one of Pat's classmates, called just before Christmas. The Williamses owned the T. H. Williams Department Store at the corner of Fifth Street and Congress Avenue; Mrs. Williams was chuckling.

"I just have to tell you this," said Miss Williams. "Knox came home from school yesterday, and said, 'I want the best Christmas present out of the store for Pat Hackerman.' "

Knox's affection for Pat was not unusual. She was a joyous child, with the charisma and magnetism that merry little girls have. She also had the beautiful gift of gratitude. I remember her fifth birthday party. One child brought Pat a child's gold-plated ring in a small square jewelry box. Pat opened the box and saw nothing but the cotton. Her face lighted up, and she exclaimed, "Oh, a little old bitty piece of cotton!" Somehow she knew that any gift, any show of love, was precious. I like to call her fey, in the best meaning of the word — enchanted and enchanting.

At nine, Pat was a lively little girl, constantly in motion. She was a climber, and could scoot higher in any tree than any boy in the neighborhood. No cabinet in the house was beyond her reach. Once she climbed up on the high kitchen counter, fell, and split her chin. Another time she fell out of a tree, and the fall knocked her out. We had to check for concussion.

Pat was gregarious. She brought everybody home with her.

58

Pat, Miracle Child

She cheerfully went to meet adventures, some planned and others not.

We often let Pat and Steve each invite a friend for an outing to the San Antonio Zoo in Brackenridge Park and to ride the paddle boats in San Marcos, topping off the day with fried chicken, biscuits and honey at Youngblood's on South Lamar Boulevard. Such outings offered opportunity for Pat's sociable and adventurous qualities to shine, as well as for Steve's to develop.

And yet, Pat, for all her tree climbing, liked pretty clothes. Sewing for her was fun. We thought she was beautiful, the way she tossed her head, the way she smiled. She had a lovely neck — the kind that was called an "Audrey Hepburn," long and swan-like.

During the summer before Pat was in the second grade, Norm and I took the children to California. Norm had a consulting job there, and we combined this with a family trip.

Just before we left Austin, I noticed a knot in Pat's neck on the right side. When we got home from the trip, I took her to our pediatrician, who said, "It's just a swollen gland, like children always get." I wasn't satisfied and took her to the kind of doctor then called an "eye, ear, nose and throat specialist." He examined the knot and said it could be tuberculosis. "But kids are always having knots in their necks," said he. "Just watch it." Mother-like, I continued to be very concerned about the knot in Pat's neck. But it never got smaller.

The next summer Pat, Steve and I rode with Norm to Baltimore. Norm left us and the car with his parents in Westminster, a small town just outside Baltimore. He continued by plane to Colby College in New Hampshire to attend the ten-day Gordon Conference for electro-chemists. The plan was for me to stay with my in-laws for another day, then drive to Crisfield, on the eastern shore of Maryland, so the children and I could spend a few days with my Uncle Nelson Coulbourn. From there I would drive on to New York, where we would spend the night in a hotel, and then continue to Lexington, Massachusetts, to the home of Herb and Greta Uhlig. Herb, who taught chemistry at Massachusetts Institute of Technology, and Norm were roommates at the Gordon Conference. I had never met Greta, but Norm said the Uhligs had two children about Pat and Steve's ages, and a baby as well.

The Time Has Come

According to plan, I drove from Westminster to Crisfield to Uncle Nelson's home. I wanted my children to see Pomphret Manor, the fourteen hundred acres our ancestors had settled three centuries before under a grant from the English king.

Uncle Nelson had always been a sustaining part of my life. He and his wife, Agnes, had no children. When I graduated from high school in Baltimore, they tried to bribe me to come live with them, offering me a red Packard convertible. But I was not of an age that found the quiet country life appealing.

My uncle had started a seafood packing company in Old Port Comfort, Virginia. He had moved the business to Crisfield, where it grew and prospered with the advent of refrigerated railway cars. So by the time the children and I visited him in 1953, he was a well-to-do lord of the manor, having bought the place from my grandfather's estate after my father decided he would rather have money.

Aunt Agnes may well have been the model for my intense interest in rebuilding and decorating houses, and in gardening. She and I wrote to each other through the years, and she sent me iris rhizomes that I planted in many Hackerman gardens. From her and the house she lived in, I learned the art of adding a room here and a room there.

The Pomphret Manor I introduced Pat and Steve to was a wonderful place, and architecturally classic in its pattern of add-ons. The first houses in America's Tidewater — and this was one — started with one room, called the kitchen, but with no fireplace. It actually was where all the living and eating went on. The cooking was done in a separate building out back, so that if a fire broke out, the living area would be safe. The next addition was "shinbone alley," built above the large room with stairs leading up to it. The ceilings were only five feet tall, and the windows were covered with priscilla curtains. Steve loved this room and slept there the nights we stayed with Uncle Nelson.

The next addition was a kind of "extended arm," a long area opening back and front from the original room. The parlor was built with bedrooms above. The final product was a large house with magnificent grounds and a mile of circular drive. Roses, tulips, irises, lilac bushes, and dozens of other blooming plants perfumed the manor and dazzled the eye.

The fifty Hereford cattle my uncle kept were more suggestive of the "Wild West" than anything at our home in Austin. Uncle Nelson took Steve riding on the tailgate of his pickup, and the image remains in my mind of Steve's little legs in his Texas cowboy boots, hanging over the edge of that truck.

A footnote to this trip: After we got back to Austin Steve refused to drink milk for a long time. He had learned at Pomphret Manor that milk did not originate in the bottles delivered to our door three times a week.

Throughout our visit we were surrounded by the love and tenderness I had learned to expect from Uncle Nelson. When we left, he filled my car with goodies from the farm, a marked map to Wilmington, and the name of a hotel there which Uncle Nelson said would be a good, safe one for me and the children on our way to Massachusetts.

Wilmington was a pleasant stop, but the next night in New York City was neither safe nor comfortable. I located a hotel room through Travelers' Aid. The assigned room was on the ninth floor, and with no air conditioning, it was terribly hot. Although the windows would open, they had no screens, and with two rambunctious children, I couldn't risk opening them. I asked for another room; the second floor wasn't much better. I didn't get much sleep.

The next morning we left in a hurry, and drove all day. We rolled into Lexington after dark, near 9:00 P.M. The children were hungry and tired. Forty years ago, roadsides had not yet become crowded with fast-food enticements.

It was with some misgivings that I rang that doorbell and met Greta Uhlig, a woman I'd never seen before.

Greta greeted us warmly. "I've saved some supper for you," she said. Thus began one of those unexpected friendships that I cherish so much.

Greta sat the children down and proceeded to put out a meal for us. Even now, I can see her standing at the kitchen sink cutting a cantaloupe and slicing it in child-bite sizes. Then she took the seeds and washed them carefully and put them in a bowl on the windowsill.

61

The Time Has Come

"Are you going to plant the seeds?" I asked.

"No, I'm going to feed them to the birds."

Greta and I were going to get along just fine!

"I don't know why my feet are so swollen," I mentioned. This had never happened to me before. My ankles were hanging over my shoes. "Perhaps it's from driving so long . . ."

"If they aren't better by morning, I'll take you to my doctor," Greta said. They weren't better in the morning, so we went to the doctor, and I learned I was pregnant. I had some news for Norm.

We had another day before the men would be home, so Greta and her children gave us a perfect introduction to Boston, its sights, and its history. She had a stroller for her baby, so we were undeterred in our choice of adventures. We went to Boston Common, where Steve was chased by a duck, much to that young man's delight.

Greta took us to a seafood place with sawdust on the floor. My children had never seen that before and exclaimed over it. We went to battlefields of the Revolutionary War, where the children chased each other and wore off some of the energy that had pent up from visiting grandparents, uncle, hotels, and the back seat of the car.

And then the conference was over; Norm came to Lexington, and we started back home, again stopping off in Baltimore.

It was there that we took Pat to see Norm's cousin, the physician. I asked him to take a look at Pat's neck. She now had two knots that we could feel. "It's probably just a swollen gland. Children have them a lot," he said. "But just as a precaution, take her to your physician in Austin when you get home."

When I took Pat to see the eye, ear, nose and throat specialist again, he repeated his suspected diagnosis that it could be glandular tuberculosis. He stuck a needle into one of the knots, withdrew some fluid, put a bandage on Pat's neck, and sent us out.

I just happened to see Dr. John Thomas' office, which was on the same floor as the specialist's. Dr. Thomas was our neighbor and friend, living just two doors from us on Sharon Lane. I took a chance on finding Dr. Thomas in and free. He listened to my story about Pat's neck and said he would stop by the house when he got home that evening. After he felt her neck he turned

62

away. Somehow I had the feeling he was avoiding my eyes; his own were hooded, half shut.

"Gene, we need to do a little test," he said. He suggested that we should take Pat to the hospital the next morning for a biopsy. She was to be at Seton by 7:00. The biopsy was scheduled for 8:00, and she would be back in her room by 9:00 or 9:30.

The knot was malignant.

"We can feel a number of these knots in her neck," Dr. Thomas told me. "A large area may be involved. We know we will have to remove her thyroid."

I must have remained calm through that terrible morning. And yet having left Pat asleep at the hospital, I returned home and went to pieces. I was pregnant, so the obstetrician, Dr. McCauley, was called. He told me to take a "good stiff drink" and try to rest. I mixed a drink and went into the bedroom, shut the door, and proceeded to lose control. I cried and screamed, threw a hand mirror across the room, and broke it.

An alarmed Addie Mae came to the door and asked if she could help. "Just don't bother me now," I told her, and continued to weep. After a while, I went upstairs to Pat's room and went to sleep in her bed.

Dr. Thomas referred us to Dr. Clifford Thorne, the Austin pediatrician with extensive experience with thyroid problems in children. Seeing the new pediatrician was necessary. When children have their thyroids removed, it prevents proper growth. Children's thyroids control growth or lack of growth, the child's weight (always high if the thyroid is absent), and how the child's bones grow.

Dr. Thorne measured Pat, including her hands and feet, estimating how large she would grow to be normally. From this information, he determined the right amount of thyroid replacement she would need.

We saw Dr. Thorne several times for checkups on her general health before she went into the hospital for the surgery.

One day, after making the rounds of the doctors, Pat and I had a soda, then went to the Varsity Theater to see "The Sound of Music." As I sat there watching the story of the Von Trapp family and listening to the haunting music, I was seized with panic. We were going to lose Pat. Then came one of the signs of hope I have learned to cling to through the years: the baby moved in my body for the first time. It was just a little flutter, but this sign of new life somehow helped me feel that Pat, too, would be all right. For the time I was at peace.

The fears would recur.

Dr. Thomas operated at Seton Hospital. Then on 26th Street, sitting back on an emerald lawn, the red-brick hospital was administered by the Sisters of Charity. The morning of Pat's surgery, the Mother Superior came to console me while I waited for Pat to come from the operating room. She said to me, "I have something I would like to give you, if you will accept it. I know you are not Catholic, but I'd like for you to have this."

She gave me a rosary in a box. I clutched it throughout the day, through the eight hours that Pat was in the operating room. Of course, I wanted that rosary. To this day I carry it in my purse. I don't go anywhere without it, the expression of another woman's faith and a symbol of prayers going up for Pat.

Members of the Sewing Group — Betsy Watt, Jean Maurer, Sylvia Lester and Ceil Matsen — and other friends, in all about thirty of my closest women friends, dropped by throughout the day, bringing Thermos bottles full of coffee. I was five months pregnant now, but my stomach was feather-light compared to the leaden weight of my heart. My friends and the coffee helped, as did my awareness of the rosary in the box.

At last the operation was over. Dr. Thomas told me it had gone well. He had removed twelve tumors from Pat's neck and shoulder, including the muscle in her neck and the jugular vein. Three of the tumors were malignant.

The nurses lifted our sleeping daughter, swathed in bandages, onto a high hospital bed and left me alone with her. A poem grew in my mind that I later wrote down.

PAT

I stood beside the waist-high bed,
And saw my first-born lying there,
Incision stretching down her neck
From ear to collar bone.
Sixty stitches closed the wound
That saved her life and broke my heart.

Pat, Miracle Child

I stayed in the hospital by Pat throughout the night, sometimes dozing, sometimes trying to read. Near 2:00 in the morning, I went downstairs looking for some coffee and ran into Dr. McCauley. "What are you doing here?" he asked. I told him about Pat's operation. Then he asked, "Where are you sleeping?" I told him I was sleeping in the chair in Pat's room. The next day he arranged to have Pat moved to a room large enough for another bed. The second night I slept beside her, close enough to hear her call me and comfortable enough to answer Dr. McCauley's requirements for the unborn baby.

After Pat's wounds healed, we made the first of many pilgrimages to Houston and M.D. Anderson Hospital. The first time Norm drove us down there. At that time Anderson Hospital was nothing more than a barracks in a muddy field on West Gray Street, a far cry from the great research hospital it is now. We met Dr. Lee Clark, the director of the hospital whom we would come to know so well, both personally and professionally. Even during that first visit, he, the cancer physician-researcher, and Norm, the scientist, discussed plans for the hospital and its potential to lead the long exploratory journeys to finding cures for cancer.

For Pat, the doctors recommended a series of radioactive iodine treatments to be administered at M.D. Anderson. After this first trip, I drove Pat to Houston, leaving Steve with Addie Mae at home.

Pat and I stayed at the Shamrock Hotel, so we could have a good place to sleep. She usually had to see the doctors for two days in a row. Hulon Black, then director of the University of Texas Development Board, called Johnnie McKetta (he and Pinky then lived in Houston) to tell the McKettas that Pat and I were staying at the Shamrock. After the first radioactive iodine treatment, when we arrived at the hotel from M.D. Anderson, the McKettas were in the lobby waiting for us.

"Gene, we came by to see if we could take you and Pat to dinner," Johnny said. Their kindness greatly touched me and made the time less lonely and frightening for both Pat and me.

Sometime during the course of the treatment, we were sent by M.D. Anderson physicians to see another Houston doctor, a specialist in the kind of cancer Pat had. He told me he found lumps under her arms, in her groin and in the other side of her neck. He recommended another massive operation on the other side of her neck.

"But if you take the muscles out of that side, she won't be able to hold her head up," I remember saying.

"She'll be alive," he said.

"What kind of life is that?" I snapped back.

I can't say I consciously made a decision then between sentencing Pat to a lifetime of immobility or death. What I did was refuse to believe what the doctor said. I refused so completely that I blocked his name from my memory until many years later, when we moved to Houston and there met him socially many times. I ignored his diagnosis and, almost in a daze, went back to the hotel to call Norm, who was on an oil rig in Oklahoma. He was working with a graduate student on a doctoral project.

I couldn't call him from the hotel room; Pat would hear. I gave Pat a dollar and asked her, "Pat, go downstairs and get a newspaper for Mama and bring it back up." She left, and I dialed the hotel room telephone. I got Norm, but was barely able to tell him the doctor had said the cancer had spread all over when I heard Pat at the door, knocking to get in. I quickly told Norm I would go home the next day.

All packed, Pat and I went to bed. I couldn't sleep. My back pain was excruciating. I was afraid I was in labor. I called the hotel doctor, who assured me I was not.

Back home in Austin, Dr. McCauley told me I had had a gall bladder attack — the only one I've ever had. Stress was pulling me apart.

Norm is stoic. Just as worried about Pat as I, he showed his concern by burying himself in even more work. Both Norm and I had to be outwardly calm. Pat needed her parents to be cheerful and unafraid.

I had outlets for my terror. Most important of all was St. David's Church and Dr. Charles Sumner, the rector, and his Healing Prayer group. That is where I went first after Pat and I returned home.

The Prayer Group worked like this. A small group — never more than ten or fifteen, sometimes fewer — went to the church

and met with Dr. Sumner. He invited us to write down the name
— only the first name — of the person we wanted the group to
pray for. On the paper we didn't write what the illness or the
problem was, only the name of the person. Then Dr. Sumner led
the prayers, reaching from time to time for a name and calling
that name. I believed — and still believe — so fervently in the power of these prayers, that if we can get enough people to pray for
one purpose, God will hear and pay attention.

Pat was known as a "miracle child," and I believe it to be true.

In my distress, in my need to know, I called on strangers.
They did not fail me. The first was Dolly Bolton. Dolly was a public figure, the wife of Paul Bolton, dean of Austin radio and television newscasters. Paul and Dolly had one child, a daughter,
Beverly Sontag. I had heard that Beverly had had thyroid cancer,
and recovered.

"Mrs. Bolton," I said on the telephone, "you don't know me,
but I need you." I poured out my story and Pat's story. I asked her
to tell me about Beverly and what had happened. She did. I asked
her how she had dealt with this. It was then she told me about
Agnes Sanford's book, *The Healing Light.*

I met Beverly, and found a beautiful young woman, a poet
who had children of her own and who had borne her ordeal with
grace and courage. Later events called again on Dolly and Beverly's courage — Beverly and Jim Sontag's son, Paul Bolton Sontag, was killed while walking along Guadalupe Street, across the
street from the University of Texas campus, in August 1966, by
Charles Whitman, the sniper from atop the University Tower.
But that is another story . . .

One afternoon I called another stranger, Dr. Bernice
"Bunk" Moore, associate director of the Hogg Foundation for
Mental Health at the University of Texas. Bunk and her husband,
Dr. Harry Moore, were a well-known team of sociologists, whose
research and personal influence built healthier psyches for thousands. So one afternoon, I called Bunk Moore. For many years
she suffered from migraine headaches, sometimes almost inca-
pacitating her with pain, and I caught her at home, resting, with
one of these headaches. Even so, she recognized the desperation

in my voice when I asked, "What should I tell Pat? She asks so many questions. How can I answer them?"

Bunk took immediate action. She arranged a three-station conference call, a conversation among Bunk, a social worker at M.D. Anderson Hospital, and me. Bunk posed the questions, and I supplied some of the details. The social worker said, "By no means tell Pat the gravity of the situation. Don't frighten her. Try to be cheerful around her and help her to lead as normal a life as possible."

I tried to follow this advice. Pat went to Girl Scout Camp that summer, where she earned her Rowing Badge even though she was missing those muscles in her neck and shoulder. Apparently the strategy was working. We would treat her as if she can do anything she had done before, and she could do it.

Remaining cheerful myself was a little harder, but thanks to continuing support from friends, even this was possible. Each day I was growing larger and larger with the new baby, even as Pat gained thirty pounds because she had no thyroid to regulate her growth. Betsy Watt of the Sewing Group made Pat a smock-type dress, buttoned down the front with fabric left over from a maternity smock made for me.

One day I was combing Pat's hair and a hunk of hair the size of a nickel fell out of her scalp in my hand. I broke down and cried. Pat's beautiful hair —

Pat and I made our regular trips to M.D. Anderson, staying usually at the Shamrock. After the radioactive iodine would be administered, we would try to do something special. Once we went to the Theater-in-the-Round, another time to the circus. During these excursions, Pat invariably needed to go to the restroom. I knew she was having iodine in which a few drops of the radioactive isotope had been placed. I knew that radioactive materials usually glowed in the dark. I also remembered that watches with faces painted with this material allowed us to tell time in the dark.

The doctors at Anderson were keeping a close watch on Pat's urine to check the progress of the radioactive isotope in the iodine treatments.

We had to keep all of Pat's urine in a gallon jug, supplied by

Pat, Miracle Child

Anderson Hospital, for twenty-four hours, returning it to the laboratory the next day. I carried this jug with me. Walking out of the theater restroom, back to our seats in the dark, with the jug hanging from one hand and Pat from the other, I giggled, wondering if we could be glowing in the dark ourselves.

Pat had three more operations — all at Seton Hospital in Austin, all done by Dr. Thomas. None was the operation that would have taken away her ability to hold up her head. We managed to conceal the physical effects of the operations with high-collared blouses and bright scarves.

*   *   *

Nine years later, on a spring evening, Mary Jane Hemperley and I sat in the balcony of the auditorium at Austin High School and watched as Pat was selected first runner-up in the Maroon Beauty Revue. Mary Jane and I clasped hands as we realized that Pat indeed was one of the most beautiful young women in Austin.

Chapter 10

Boys Are Different

The years 1953 and 1954 are now shrouded in a kind of haze. Pat's four operations were over and I no longer had to make the long, progressively more exhausting drive to Houston. With each trip, it had seemed that I, with my swollen belly, was less able to fit behind the steering wheel.

The winter's hail and snow flurries had passed. I was much absorbed with Pat, watchful that we give her plenty of love but not spoil her or take away her sense of playfulness and joy.

One midnight in the middle of March, in spite of a breach delivery, Sally had hammered her way into the world. A chubby, lovable baby, Sally was the kind you liked to hold and cuddle. She was the one of whom my friend Betsy said, "Gene, you really hit the jackpot on this one." So on the one hand there was Pat, needing attention, and on the other, the baby, also needing attention.

In the middle was our wonderful, good, bright little boy, Steve. Seven years old, he gave us no trouble, seeming to understand the crises we were going through.

Or so I thought.

When his second-grade teacher at Casis called me and asked for a conference, I thought it was to go over his schoolwork — a routine conference.

"I notice," she said, "that Steve is very quiet. That's unusual for a seven-year-old boy. He does his usual outstanding work, is obedient and listens. But he's *too quiet.*"

70

Boys are Different

She suggested that we make an appointment at the Child Guidance Center to see if the professional counselors there could get to the bottom of Steve's reserve.

After a few weeks of regular sessions at the center, with separate sessions for Steve and for me, a counselor told me: "Steve thinks you like girls better than boys."

I was stunned. *That can't possibly be true,* was my first thought. Then I realized what Steve was seeing. Pat, whose thyroid replacement was still being adjusted, was often cold, so I took her into bed with me, holding her close to keep her warm. I also held the new baby to feed her every four hours, day and night. So what Steve saw was Mother with a girl child embraced in her arms time after time, and a little boy standing aside.

"What can I do?" I asked.

"Do something with *just Steve,*" the counselor suggested. "Ask him what he wants to do for a whole day with you."

I talked with Steve and he said he wanted to go fishing! Neither he nor I nor anyone else in our family had *ever* fished, but I was game and Steve was adamant.

I told Norm that Steve and I were going on a little trip. I found someone who would take care of the baby and Pat. I had found a guest ranch about an hour from Austin with a stream for fishing, horses to ride, and a camplike atmosphere. Ideal, I thought. Bar-K Ranch, here we come.

Steve and I got settled in our cabin, then went seeking the equipment for fishing. Having never fished in my life, what did I know? We rented a pole and bought a can of worms and, feeling professionally equipped, followed directions to the creek and settled ourselves comfortably at the edge of the dock, with our legs dangling over the edge.

Taking a worm in two fingers, and draping it over the fishhook, I thought, *This isn't so bad.* Of course, it fell off before Steve could sink the line in the water. So I draped another worm over the hook. This went on for some minutes while we lost half the worms.

A gentleman sitting a few yards from us, watching this strange performance, broke the silence.

"Honey," he said, "don't you know how to put a worm on a hook?"

"No, sir," I said, "we haven't done this before."

He showed me how to thread the hook through the worm, end to end (this *was* bad). I gritted my teeth and did it. Steve began to catch fish, lots of them. But they were very small and had to be thrown back. I took the fish off the hook carefully, so they wouldn't get hurt too badly. But I didn't know about their fins. They were *sharp,* and my hands were soon scratched and lacerated.

I suggested to Steve that he might want to put the worms on the hook.

"No," he said, "you do it."

The bitter bile of nausea rose in my throat and I decided this was a bunch of stuff. Enough of this fishing.

"Do you want to stop?" I asked Steve.

"Sure," he answered, with relief in his voice.

"What do you want to do now?" I asked.

"Could we go home?"

And so we did.

* * *

Steve had an afternoon newspaper route when he was in junior high school. As soon as he got home from school and consumed his peanut butter sandwich, he began rolling papers. In the spring and summer, he delivered the *Austin Statesman* from his bicycle, but in the wintertime, when dark descended before he could get through, I'd take him in the station wagon, with him sitting on the extended tailgate as I crept along at a snail's pace. Sometimes I helped him roll the papers — not that he needed the help, but because I wanted to be close to this boy child growing up so fast and so quietly in the midst of this talkative family.

Sometimes we talked as we snapped the rubber bands around the rolled papers and tossed them into the back of the station wagon, but most often we just worked together.

I'd drive slowly as he sat in the back and threw the papers into the yards. Some of his customers demanded that the paper be "porched," as Steve explained. I'd wait with the engine running while he ran to do this.

The ink from the papers etched itself into our hands, smudged up our clothes, and left fingerprints on anything we touched. Most of it could be scrubbed out in the washing machine and the bathroom sink, but I began to notice that Steve apparently wasn't washing his face when he bathed. Ink smudges were all over his chin and cheeks. One morning as he was hurrying to get off to school, I said, "Steve, your face is still dirty. If you can't get it clean, I'm going to wash it for you." This was a dire threat for an adolescent boy!

"Mama," he said, "I've been trying to tell you for months. That's my beard!"

I was stunned. This boy-child, gawky as a young colt, wrists and ankles protruding out of jacket and jeans, was becoming a man!

*   *   *   *   *

Boys are different from girls, and as my friend, Bunk Moore, so often said, *viva le difference.* But the obvious physical differences are not what I mean. Boys are more *vulnerable* than girls. This revelation came to me when I took Steve to Casis School for the first time. When I dropped off the girls at Casis, they happily skipped up the walkway, with their pigtails or curls bouncing and their little short skirts flipping to their movements. When they met their classmates, they yelled, "Hi," and happily went into the school, laughing and chattering.

I noted it was different with boys. They got out of their mothers' cars more slowly. Their necks seemed so long and thin jutting up from their sweaters. Their hair was short-cropped. They had no place to hide their vulnerability. They were less likely to skip to meet the day and their friends. When a little boy encountered another, he greeted him with a shove — a friendly shove, but a shove nonetheless.

Girls are more social. A girl, almost from babyhood, has nurturing tasks to attend to — dolls to dress, tidying up to do. Girls mature faster, and their small muscles work earlier, so they can manipulate needle and thread. Boys, on the other hand, run and hammer, paint a wide swath as they exercise their large muscles.

The Time Has Come

This difference is less sexist and social than many people believe; it has to do with physical development.

I watched Steve grow with a very real tug at my heart, a desire to shield him from life's tragedies, even the small ones. I understand that this is a common maternal feeling toward boys. I watched Steve grow from the vulnerable little boy with the long neck going forth to comradely shove one of his peers, to an extra-tall, thin junior high schooler.

Social life at O. Henry Junior High was active, with the children — especially the girls — rushing toward adulthood. Steve was particularly interested in one of the more popular girls. He confided that he wanted to invite her to the O. Henry dance. As the date neared, I realized that he had been procrastinating.

"Have you invited her yet?" I asked one afternoon.

"Not yet."

"Why don't you call her now?" As Steve walked to the telephone, I saw again the little shy second grader, with his long neck, moving toward a difficult task of socializing.

He came back into the kitchen where I was wrapping hot dogs in waxed paper, and said, "Someone else already asked her." My heart was filled with compassion.

"Don't worry," I said lamely. "Ask her earlier, next time." Somehow, words of maternal wisdom are never there when you need them!

As a little boy, Steve had a consuming wanderlust. It may have extended only eight blocks or so, but that was much too far for a five-year-old. His favorite toy at the time was a little car that he could sit in. It was run by muscle power, Steve's pumping the pedals under the hood. He could get around fast, covering hill and dale, as it turned out.

Pauline Watt lived on Stamford Lane near the firehouse, at least eight blocks from our home on Sharon Lane. Pauline had twin boys, who, of course, were magnets to Steve. One afternoon Pauline called and said, "Gene, I have an extra boy here. I'm holding him for you."

I jumped into the car and rushed to Stamford Lane. On the way up the walk, I paused to break a switch off Pauline's hedge.

Boys Are Different

Steve then and there received his first and only corporal punishment from me. I gave him one or two stinging whacks on his leg.

Steve's pedal car landed him in another scrape. I had invited a number of women to have coffee with me in the garden on a certain morning. The yard man had mowed, trimmed, clipped, and swept until everything looked perfect.

My picnic table and benches looked, I thought, a little shabby so I scurried to the paint store the afternoon before party day. I spent the afternoon painting the table and benches a wonderful dark green. Steve wanted to paint his car, so I poured some paint into an old can and gave him a brush. He worked the rest of the afternoon turning the red car green. By the time he finished, I too was through and had cleaned my brushes. Steve's paint can was essentially empty, so I left it and his worn-out brush in the paint can sitting under a tree, to be disposed of the next morning.

Steve was barefooted and had paint on the soles of his feet. He had paint in his hair, on one eyebrow, all over his hands and face. I cleaned him off with turpentine and bathed him. He ate his supper and went early to bed. I did, too. I was bushed.

It was still dark when I woke to a little voice saying, "Mama, Mama, wake up." Somehow I knew it was Pat.

"Go away, honey," I said, "let Mama sleep just a little bit longer."

She persisted. "Mom, you have to get up. Steve is painting the front of the house."

And so he was. On the day of my party, with a sticky paint brush, he had painted as high as he could reach, the whole front of the wing of the house. It was a mess . . . a green mess.

"Put down that brush," I said, with a strained, determined calm. "Get upstairs and don't come down until I come to get you."

With steel wool, turpentine and Old Dutch Cleanser, I scrubbed the front of my house. Pat stayed out of the way, seeing how angry I was.

Of course, the anger passed. I went upstairs and talked to him. He didn't get a spanking, but I believe he *was* sorry that he had had so much fun painting the front of the house.

The mail was delivered twice a day — once in the morning and once in the afternoon. While I was scrubbing the boards, the postman came up the walk and delivered a package from my friend, Rita Johns, then living in Turkey. Her gift was a copper-washed pewter container which I treasure to this day. Every time I polish it, I think about Steve and his Tom Sawyer prank.

By the time the ladies came for coffee, the front of the house looked presentable. However, I served the coffee with green-rimmed fingernails.

Another adventure in the Steve lore occurred while I was working in the legislature as a secretary to a representative. I earned only ten dollars a day, but could usually go home by mid-afternoon, as soon as I had finished the day's work. This particular afternoon, Addie Mae met me at the door in tears.

"I can't find him," she sobbed. "I can't find him. I've been to Westenfield Park. I've been everywhere, but there's no Steve."

I panicked. Addie Mae and I went back to the park together. That was the place he would most likely be. The children and I spent many mornings there in the summers, and often the playground leaders went home with us for lunch during their noonday break.

City workers were putting in new drainage pipes, big ones that a child could stand up in and crawl through. We looked in every pipe. Still no Steve.

We went back home, and I called the police. "We've lost our little boy," I told the dispatcher. Within a few minutes a policeman was on the steps, ringing the doorbell.

Just behind the policeman stood Steve Hackerman.

"*Where* have you been, young man?" I asked.

"At Mr. Sims' house," said Steve. (The Simses lived two doors from us.) "He lets me watch television," Steve went on, "and you won't. I came home to see what the policeman wanted at our house."

The policeman was wonderful. When I apologized for calling him, he said, "That's all right, lady, it happens all the time."

Chapter 11

The Empty Crib

The 1950s remain a cliché of happy times, of family serenity, though the chill of cold war was descending over the world, and McCarthyism spread unease throughout American academia and the arts. The early fifties were especially happy for me because Pat's cancer seemed to have disappeared, and she was learning to live gracefully with the scars on her neck. Sally, who had come into the world in 1954, stared at it with the most beautiful dark brown eyes I had ever seen. I mentioned this to Dr. McCauley, and he said he had delivered more than 1,200 babies, and had never seen one before with black eyes. (Usually newborn babies have blue eyes that change in a few weeks.)

During the period just after Sally was born and for a few months afterwards, Steve and I grew closer because we went through counseling at the Child Guidance Center. Through this, Steve came to understand mother love and how he was just as important to me as his sisters.

I was a very happy young mother.

In June of 1955 I became pregnant again. This added to my joy. Physically I always felt very good when I was pregnant, and this time was no exception.

The baby was due in late February of 1956. I had no difficulty during the first six months of the pregnancy. About that time I started occasionally spotting, but I gave it little thought. I had had miscarriages, but they had come much earlier than the sixth month of pregnancy.

The Time Has Come

Of course, I consulted my doctor. He agreed there was nothing to worry about; the baby was big. He did suggest that for the next couple of months I stay off my feet as much as possible and not drive a car. The baby was lying in a transverse position, but the doctor said it would turn when the time came.

Pat was nearly fourteen. Dr. McCauley suggested that I apply for a driver's permit for her, so she could take Steve to Casis, Sally to Inez Jeffery's preschool, and herself to O. Henry. This helped a lot.

After the seventh month of pregnancy, I made trips to see Dr. McCauley. Everything seemed to be fine. I gained quite a bit of weight — probably because I stayed in bed as often as I could.

February had come and almost gone. Norm and I went one Saturday night to Jack and Evelyn Myers' house to play poker. We played for an hour or so, and I felt some pains which seemed to me might be the beginning of labor. We finished the hand, and I decided it would be wise for me to go home. The baby was overdue. Having had three babies, all weighing more than eight pounds, I felt this one might just pop out quickly and with no difficulty.

We got home, and the pains stopped. I went to bed. On Sunday morning I felt fine. No more pains. Toward evening I had no pain, but an eerie sense of silence engulfed me. It was a silence like that when the power in the house goes off. I heard the little noises that the power drowns out.

I felt no movement from the baby, and missed it. Even the tiny fluttery movements that I had barely noticed were gone.

During the night I got up and went to sleep on the couch. It was 4:00 in the morning. I felt all right, just strange. I didn't want to disturb Norm or the children, and I didn't want to call Dr. McCauley at that hour.

I did call his office at 7:30 in the morning. "Are you having labor pains?" the nurse asked.

"No," I answered, "but I feel strange."

She suggested I come on in.

I drove to Dr. McCauley's office. He came in after his rounds. I was lying on the table.

"I thought the baby was coming Saturday night, but then the pains went away," I explained to him.

The Empty Crib

He put his stethoscope on my stomach. Then he walked away and stood silently looking out the window, for a few minutes, with his back turned toward me.

"I think you need to go to the hospital right away. We need to get this baby started," he said.

I told him I couldn't do that today, that I had to go to the grocery, and see about the children.

"No," he said. "You need to get to the hospital now." He turned to the nurse, and said to her, "Get hold of Norman Hackerman. Tell him to get down here as fast as he can."

Norm walked from the university to the doctor's office. He and Dr. McCauley had a conversation out of my hearing.

Norm took me to Seton Hospital. Everybody seemed in a hurry. They gave me a shot that sent me into a kind of twilight zone. Norm and Dr. McCauley stood by the bed as something was being dripped into my arm.

The baby had been in transverse position, but had apparently turned on Saturday night. Through the haze, I heard the doctor tell Norm, "It's a good thing she is living in this generation. If she were in a wagon train, they'd have to toss both her and the baby out." That's all I remember for a while.

The next thing I knew I was sitting up in bed. Norm and Dr. McCauley came in together and told me the baby was born dead.

"We'll get you another baby," Norm said.

Neither he nor the doctor told me if the baby was a boy or a girl. When the nurse came in, I asked her.

"She was a beautiful ten-pound girl," she said. "I'm so sorry."

They moved me from the maternity floor to the surgical floor. I stayed in the hospital for a week. I walked the halls, and several times a day went to the nursery window, looking at the babies, feeling my grief — but never really resolving it. I felt I had to do this. I just had to get used to live babies before I went home to my children.

Norm buried the baby, unnamed. Thirty-five years later, he told me where she is buried, our beautiful unknown daughter.

A few weeks after I returned home and took up my life again, Norm and I went to an open house at Anne and Harold

The Time Has Come

Robinson's. As we stood on the steps leading down into the living room, someone called out, "Gene, what did you have?"

A sea of faces all turned and looked at me, standing on those steps. I almost said, "A dead baby."

Somehow, I answered, "A girl."

*   *   *

When I went back to see Dr. McCauley for my six-week checkup, I said to him, "Mac, I haven't received a bill from you yet or I've mislaid it."

He replied, looking straight at me, "I never send a bill when the baby has died."

*   *   *

Norm had promised me, "We'll get you another baby." I held him to his promise.

On December 13, 1958, two and a half years later, I held a beautiful baby girl, our Katy — the promise fulfilled.

Chapter 12

Girls Are Different, Too

arge sections of time from 1952 until 1958 are
blocked out of my mind, years that were filled with
vast emotional swings, from the depths of despair
to radiant happiness. These years were swathed in
mist that occasionally cleared. Most of 1952 I vaguely remember.
Pat had four cancer operations and I was pregnant with Sally.
The mist disappeared for a while and the sun came out again
when Sally was born. But the mist and fog closed in again when
the newborn baby died. Then the sun burst through two and a
half years later with the arrival of Katy.

While boys and girls are different in the ways they grow and
socialize, I found that our three daughters also were as individual
as three people could be. This is easy to understand. They lived in
different times, grew up in different houses, and had different
parents.

Pat is ten years older than Sally. Sally is five years older than
Katy. Pat is blonde. Sally is brunette, and Katy is somewhere in
between. Pat was born in Virginia and migrated with us to Texas
when she was less than two years old. Both Sally and Katy were
born in Seton Hospital while we were living on Sharon Lane, but
Katy spent most of her growing up years in President's Houses at
the University of Texas and Rice.

Pat is outgoing and gregarious, lovable and funny. Sally is
shyer, more self-contained. She is regal and beautiful. Katy is intense and brilliant, dedicated to perfection.

81

The Time Has Come

Their talents — considerable for each of them — were markedly different from each other's. Their dispositions and socialization patterns also were unique. Pat always had a wide circle of friends, while Sally had two or three to whom she was fiercely loyal. Katy had competitive friends — both boys and girls. She played tennis to win. In fact, Katy has always played to win in whatever she undertakes.

The differences in our daughters became more marked as they matured. Pat wanted to be a member of Chi Omega Sorority, and so she was. Sally, ten years later, was on campus during a much different time; social consciousness rather than social activities were more the order of the day. So Sally asked me to help her respond to the sororities' invitations, thanking them but declining. Five years later, sororities were again popular, and Katy pledged Kappa Kappa Gamma.

Pat's teenage clothing ran to circular poodle skirts, saddle shoes, and beehive hairdos. Sally's ran to granny dresses and granny glasses, but no ponchos! She wore her lovely black hair long and shining to her shoulders. Sally was never a hippie, but her idea of dressing up was a skirt and sweater with a Peter Pan collar peeking above the sweater.

All three of the girls were Junior Helping Hand debutantes in Austin, but Katy was the only one who was an Allegro debutante in Houston. Pat was married and Sally declined the invitation to be one.

Although all three of these girls had different tastes as far as sororities, clothing and activities were concerned, all of them were fond of boys. However, all three of them chose different modes of getting married. Pat was married by a Reformed rabbi, Levi Olan, at that time a member of the Board of Regents of the University of Texas. She was marrying a Jewish man who went to school with her at UT. Her wedding was at home (Sharon Lane), complete with canopy and the breaking of the wine glass.

Sally, on the other hand, wanted the plainest, simplest marriage possible, not to be performed by a man of the cloth. She wanted the ceremony held in the President's House at Rice. The vows were written by her and the man she married, Dennis Myers, and the ceremony was performed by Judge Blanton.

82

Girls Are Different, Too

The last year we were at Rice, Katy chose to be married in the Rice Chapel and had a traditional wedding.

So our three daughters grew up to be women of strength, each different, but all sure of themselves.

Part 2

Chapter 13

A Tale of Two Universities

 ifty years ago, when Norman Hackerman and Gene
Allison Coulbourn joined hands in Holy matrimo-
ny, they began what they hoped would be a joyous
scamper through the campuses of academia.

It didn't turn out that way! The marriage turned out fine, but
the "joyous scamper" became an exhilarating, hilarious, ridiculous, and sometimes hazardous ride on a roller coaster, with
stops at seats of government in the United States and the capitals
of the world.

This ride had its home base at two fine universities: the University of Texas at Austin and Rice University, listed in the order
in which they came into my life. These two universities provided
me with a unique opportunity to look at the job of a university
president's wife from two completely different angles. Our first
seven years were at the University of Texas at Austin, a large and
prestigious public university, and the last fifteen at Rice University, a small and elite private university.

Here follow some observations.

My experience of the University of Texas was characterized
by three differing social forces. Having come up through the
ranks, I knew 1,500 faculty members by their first names. Also,
being involved, by necessity, with the Texas political system,
since this large state university is situated in the capital, we were
often included in the social life surrounding the Capitol. Finally,
we were thrust into the national scene by a United States president who called Central Texas and Austin his home, and our in-

volvement with the First Family broadened the scope of our activities.

At Rice University, on the other hand, I entered as the president's wife, and so I knew no one. Our life at Rice meant becoming involved in the cosmopolitan, explosively growing Houston, with its consular corps of thirty-six members, and its expansive cultural and social life replete with opera, symphony, ballet, art museums, and NASA. We were invited to space shuttle lift-offs, and experienced frequent visits from European royalty.

*   *   *

Dr. David Riesman, the Harvard sociologist, has scrutinized university communities and their inhabitants, and has considerably enhanced understanding of these societies. He is responsible for encouraging me to think about the role of a university president's wife. He asked me to review his paper, "Some Observations on the President's Spouse: Hazards and Opportunities."

Particularly interesting were his insights into how often university presidents' wives suffered isolation, loneliness, and other role-related pressures. One of his most vivid examples was that of a wife so unhappy in her position that he suggested, "If this college loses its remarkable president, it will be because of his wife."

David Riesman has a valid point. There are indeed great public pressures imposed on presidents' wives. And the pressure doesn't end with public responsibilities, since presidents' wives are often involved in complex family structures, including teenagers, young adults, and, yes, even small children.

For more than twenty-two years (1963–1985) I constantly led two lives: my university/public life and my private family life. Each consumed enormous portions of my time. Eighteen-hour days were the rule, not the exception.

The two lives ran parallel. On the one hand I had a family — four children, their spouses, and nine grandchildren (there was always a crib in the President's House!). As wife, mother, and grandmother, I managed to attend and/or plan and produce university graduations, high school graduations, debutante parties, rehearsal dinners, weddings and grandchildren's births (all but one). Simultaneously, I participated in all university activities

A Tale of Two Universities

— entertaining faculty, students, alumni, members of governing boards and their spouses, and friends of the universities — all in the President's House.

The University of Texas Phase

Those years (1963–1970) were full of student unrest across the country, and the University of Texas was not immune. They were years of assassination, dissent, and political upheaval. A president from Texas was in the White House, and we lived in Austin, the state capital, with Texas governors, legislators, and officials in residence.

This was the campus where I had already spent eighteen years before Norm became president. I knew many of the faculty by their first names. I had had or still had their children in Brownie troops or Cub Scout troops or Bible study classes. I had held their wives' hands when they had babies, and they mine when I had my children. We had shared good times and sad times. This was the campus where I had literally grown up, having arrived there as a young bride. The faculty knew our children, two of whom were just entering college there. I knew this campus, and it knew me — but I knew *nothing* about being a president's wife.

There is a training course for the wives of first-time presidents to which universities send their new first ladies. I am sure Texas did not send me because I had already acted as department chairman's wife, dean's wife, and vice-president's wife. Even so, there were many things I didn't know, and when Norm became president, Pat Maguire, my long-time friend and editor of the alumni magazine, the *Alcalde,* asked me what she could do to help.

"Get me a book on academic protocol," I answered. She did, and wrote this inscription, "To Gene Hackerman, who needs it less than anyone I know."

She was wrong. The experiences in this cat-bird seat are unique, and the buck does stop here.

I learned early that the ground you walk on often seems shaky and that, more often than not, the situations in which you find yourself are a bit sticky. I often remarked to friends that I

89

was walking on Jell-O. When asked how things were going, I sometimes replied, "A normal day in the glue factory." I learned that if you lose your sense of humor, you cannot survive. Fortunately, I have a good sense of humor. I have kept track not only of hazardous and world-shaking events, but of the amusing ones too, those in which I have been privileged to participate because I was married to a university president.

My children were in the university, in junior high school, and in elementary school. At the time Norm became president, the younger girls were twelve and seven. This public world, this life in a goldfish bowl, affects not only wives, but also children.

So there I stood, a president's wife, with four children and an extremely busy husband, on the threshold of the most exciting life a person could have.

We were invited to parties given by the governor and his lady. We danced and sipped champagne at inaugural balls. We were entertained by state officials, and we entertained them. But just when I began to feel important, something always happened to remind me how ridiculous we all are at one time or another.

One cool, crisp fall morning, I took my two younger children to their separate schools, returned home, washed dishes, and made beds. Bathed and dressed, I put on my hat and white gloves. The governor's wife, Mrs. Price Daniel, had invited me to pour morning coffee at the Governor's Mansion. In those days we wore hats and white gloves to coffees and teas. I got into my car, and it wouldn't start. At this point, the milkman came up the drive. He tried to start the car for me. Nothing happened. He kindly offered me a ride, so Mrs. Hackerman, president's wife, rode to town and up to the Governor's Mansion, standing in the front of a milk truck, perfectly attired in her tasteful hat and crisp white gloves.

This illustrates, I believe, the necessity to improvise, make do, and solve problems. In this job, one has to. There is no one to do it for you. A state university depends on the state officials for its livelihood, so one tries to be as accommodating as possible. One learns to show up, when invited, to their important events, and, in turn, to invite them to functions at the university — and to remember their names.

A Tale of Two Universities

We were privileged to attend several dinners in the White House, one of which was a state dinner for the president of Italy. The Protocol Office called from Washington to tell us what to wear, when to arrive, what sort of limousine to arrive in, and what would happen when we arrived.

I was so excited that two plain, ordinary citizens were dining in the White House with the president that I ate virtually nothing. After dinner, there was a performance of "The Man of La Mancha," followed by champagne and dancing in the foyer.

I felt I looked smashing in my long, pale blue sheath, covered with a silver net cage — the holes in the net the size of nickels. I danced with a number of partners, and became attached to the last one. For a while I thought I might take him home with me. He was an admiral or a captain or whatever, gorgeous in the regalia of full naval dress uniform: gold buttons and braid. We were joined to each other with gold buttons and silver net.

When our dance was over, he bowed graciously. As he straightened up, moving backward, I moved forward. Startled, I moved backward, and he came forward. We did this several times before we realized that his gold buttons were caught in the holes of my silver net. After what seemed an interminable time, with much fumbling and muttering, bowing and bending, the officer unhooked his buttons. We both moved away as rapidly as we could to opposite sides of the dance floor!

*   *   *

During this time in our lives, the White House asked us to set up a luncheon to entertain the United Nations ambassadors. These ambassadors, seventy-five strong, were making several stops in Texas. Their schedule (and, necessarily, ours) included dinner and dancing on the expansive patio at San Antonio's HemisFair. The dinner was hosted by the United States ambassador to Australia, Edward Clark, and Mrs. Clark, on a Friday evening, July 3. The ambassadors would board a bus to Austin Saturday morning, the fourth, for a luncheon hosted by Norm and me. President Johnson had asked us to have the luncheon in the Rare Books Room in the University Tower. The logistics of getting hot food up there took some planning, since no kitchen is there.

91

The Time Has Come

Our guests spoke French, German, Dutch, Swahili, Chinese, Spanish, and Portuguese. I had invited professors and spouses who spoke those languages, asking them each to host a table where the majority of guests were speaking the same language.

On Friday, I set up the round tables for ten, checked the plans for keeping the food hot, and had centerpieces delivered and placed on tables. At 3:30 that afternoon, I set the thermostat on fifty degrees to keep the flowers fresh overnight, turned off the lights, locked the doors, and drove across campus to pick up my husband from his chemistry lecture. In the car, I had his evening clothes and mine, and our overnight gear.

By 4:00 we were on our way to San Antonio to dine and dance in our finery, secure in the knowledge that everything was under control for the luncheon the next day.

Ambassador and Mrs. Clark were courtly and charming as they hosted the elegant dinner for the ambassadors. Also attending were the University of Texas Board of Regents and other university and state officials. The clock approached midnight, and as I danced with the chairman of the UT Board, Frank Erwin, I heard him ask, "Gene, you *did* remember a gift from the university for each of the ambassadors, didn't you?"

I turned where I always turn. "Please, God, what do I do now?" And at that moment, the director of the University Press, Frank Wardlaw, danced into my view.

"Why, of course," I replied to the chairman of the board. At that moment, my husband came to claim me, and we returned to our table.

I went to speak to Frank Wardlaw, who, only a few days before, had sent me, hot off the University Press, a beautiful portfolio containing individual prints of the Spanish missions painted by Texas artist Buck Schiwetz. I asked Frank if he had any more portfolios of the Spanish Missions available.

"Sure," he said. "How many do you need?"

"Seventy-five."

"No problem."

With a grateful hug for Frank, I proclaimed my thanks and said, "I'll pick them up early tomorrow morning at the Press." (That would have been Saturday.)

92

A Tale of Two Universities

At this point, it was, "Down girl; no way. Tomorrow is the Fourth of July. Nobody there. Building's locked Saturday, Sunday and Monday."

At 5:00 A.M. on July 4, I left my sleeping husband in San Antonio and hit the road to Austin. At 6:30, I was at my typewriter at Meadowbrook (the President's House). At 7:00, I was taking a lovely relaxing bath. At 9:00, hot curlers removed and face on, I leisurely dressed and had a cup of tea. At 10:00, I arrived at the Rare Books Room, bearing assorted items. At 11:00, guests arrived to see tables sparkling with crystal and silver, beautiful flowers and smiling hosts. As I stood beside my husband, I slipped the paper I had typed into his hand and said, "The gift is over there," nodding to my old painting easel next to his chair at our table. The last thing I truly remember is hearing Norm reading my note, saying, "Honored guests, we want each of you to have a gift to remember your trip to Texas. On this easel is a portfolio of paintings of the Spanish missions in Texas by the Texas painter, Buck Schiwetz. As you can see, it is large and bulky, especially to carry on a plane. So we have arranged to send each of you one of the portfolios to your home address."

* * *

Dealing with the political power in the White House is indeed an awesome prospect. We had the president and First Lady in our home (the President's House at the University of Texas) on several occasions. With them, of course, were the Secret Service, the governor, and other ranking Texas officeholders. The sight of the president close up always seemed to stun the maids, cooks, and others who helped to entertain him. On one occasion, the person opening the door became so excited that she left the door, ran down the steps, grabbed the president's hand, and kissed it over and over, saying, "I've always wanted to shake your hand."

On another occasion, we had a dinner for Distinguished Alumni, one of whom was Ron Ely, the then-current Tarzan. President and Mrs. Johnson were coming, the governor, a United States senator, and other distinguished guests. Limousines with flags, accompanied by police with sirens wailing, arrived and unloaded their passengers.

As the guests came up the walk, I could hear rustling in the

93

trees above them. I investigated when the guests were safely indoors. To my astonishment, the trees were full of neighborhood children waiting to see — who else, Tarzan! At that moment Ely arrived and the neighborhood rang with the roar of young, would-be Tarzans — including my own Katy. There are so many things that university presidents' wives get to do and see!

During the Texas University years there was the time I lost my petticoat at the head table sitting near the president of the United States, and the time I spent part of the day with the movie idol of my girlhood, flying over fields and fields of Texas wildflowers. I was invited to dinner in a funeral home, to lunch in a graveyard, and to dinner in a submerged atomic submarine — and I went to all!

I also experienced stressful events, frightening occasions and great sadnesses — a shooting from the Tower at the university, assassinations of public figures, and the rumbles of student discontent. At this time the climate of violence was felt all across the country in universities. We had two young female children. We took them to school and picked them up. Our high visibility (on television news virtually every night) prompted the campus police to put a walkie-talkie in the house.

At one particular time the Students for a Democratic Society (SDS) was determined to hold its national meeting on the Forty Acres. Norm gathered together a coalition of conservative, moderate and more radical professors, as well as clergy from the churches which ringed the campus, and *together* these people were able to find *non-university* space for SDS to have its meeting.

After the meeting was over, Norm asked me to plan a dinner at the President's House for the thirty people and their spouses, and I did. The morning of the dinner, I had a call from Maryland saying that Norm's father had died, and that Norm, also, had been told.

He came in a half-hour later, and we grieved together for a short while. I asked if he would like for me to call everyone and cancel the dinner.

"No," he said, "it took lots of hard work to get these people together; many had never spoken to each other before. We can't throw it away now. Just give me a little time alone."

94

A Tale of Two Universities

So we had the dinner, and I watched this man greeting and talking with every member of the group, never mentioning his own grief.

I also sat at an ROTC review, enclosed on three sides with buildings, the fourth with spectator stands. I sat with several administrators in the stands as we watched Norm standing in a Jeep being driven around the quadrangle. As the ride started, one administrator said to me, "There is a man in that window with a gun. I want you to follow me out, slowly and carefully." I did — not knowing whether Norm or someone else would be shot.

There were threatening, nasty phone calls — some with foul language I had never heard before in my life. Threatening letters also arrived on occasion. I remember one night my husband told me to take the girls upstairs and lock the doors at the top of the stairs.

I also sat in the snow on the steps of the Senate side of the Capitol in Washington for Kennedy's inauguration and heard his famous words, "Ask not what your country can do for you, but what you can do for your country."

I truly had a ringside seat at history.

The Rice University Phase

When my husband told me that the Rice University Board of Trustees wanted him to be president of Rice, I behaved like General Custer's army at Little Big Horn: "Hey, General, I don't want to go." Not because it was Rice, but because I had finally got the hang of being a president's wife at the University of Texas and didn't want to start over. I didn't want to learn a new faculty, a new city, new alumni, and other support groups.

But we did, and I did.

Soon after the move, a Houston newspaper reporter interviewed me about the "duties and responsibilities" of being a university First Lady. An interesting question, because no job description exists for the wife of a university president.

"I don't think there are any duties," I answered. "I don't think there are any responsibilities. I'm not dedicated to Rice University, wasn't dedicated to the University of Texas, or to any

95

other university. My dedication is to Norman Hackerman. I do believe very strongly, though, that any academic wife ought to be involved in what goes on, on campus.

"It is just as important for the wife of an assistant professor to be interested in her husband's university and her husband's work as it is for the wife of the university's president."

In 1970, when we arrived in Houston and at Rice University, I knew no one at all. It didn't take long, however, to get acquainted. At Rice, we lived on the campus and all I had to do was walk a few steps to be in the middle of campus life.

I arrived in Houston in a blinding rainstorm, to move into a President's House that I had worked on all summer to make it just right for entertaining Norm's academic colleagues at Rice, the students, and the alumni, as well as our fellow Houstonians.

Not long after we moved in, I found myself engaged in hand-to-hand combat with the scores of birds that called the trees around the President's House their home. And soon I was engaged in rounds of activities with students and faculty — cheering all Rice athletic teams, but with a special emphasis on women's athletics. It was during our years at Rice that women began receiving athletic scholarships and the recognition they deserve.

Because Rice was patterned after the great universities of Europe, the Board of Trustees sent our family to Europe to visit those universities, to become acquainted with the models that the founders of Rice had in mind. Norm attended meetings at all those universities while the girls and I were provided with a car and driver to show us the sights.

*   *   *

Although I knew no one when I arrived at Rice, soon the faculty and their spouses became my friends. We shared happy times at Rice, glittering occasions when world and national figures spoke on campus and truly gave students what I like to call "a vision of greatness." The President's House was the focal point for social events on campus honoring these visitors. Among them were Henry Kissinger, Lyndon Johnson, Margaret Mead, Secretary of the Treasury William Simon, Buckminster Fuller, Walter Cronkite, Harrison Salisbury, James Michener, and many others.

A Tale of Two Universities

Houston is a major art, music, medical and cultural center, and we were participants in the life of the city. Many of the leaders of business, industry and the arts in Houston were alumni of Rice, and continued their support and interest in the university.

Rice benefactors included such stellar individuals as Ima Hogg; George and Alice Brown; Oveta Culp Hobby and her son, Lieutenant Governor William P. Hobby, Jr.; and Hugh and Betty Liedtke. Norm and I were invited by the Liedtkes to go to the Galapagos Islands, an unforgettable adventure for me who by book and map had followed Darwin to the beginnings of his theory of evolution. It was a great thrill to take this voyage of discovery.

We played cards with the Browns and Oveta Culp Hobby. I had long admired Mrs. Hobby, who was commander of the Women's Army Corps (WAC) during World War II and whose accomplishments as a newspaper executive and mother of outstanding children (Lieutenant Governor Hobby and Jessica Hobby Catto) made her a model for the great strides women of Texas have made in politics and public life.

Parallel with the Rice activities, big happenings were going on in our family. Sally and Katy were graduating from high school, having debutante parties, engagement announcement parties, and weddings. Pat returned home to Texas after her marriage broke up, and she also remarried and lived in Houston while we were at Rice. Grandchildren were being born and adored.

*   *   *

Another question the Houston reporter asked me was, "What is it like to live most of your life on display?"

"I hope that people will look beneath the surface to see there's a person here, not just a figurehead," I answered. While I still insist there are no rules for a university president's wife, I do believe I was always aware that I was closely identified with the university and I probably subconsciously tried never to do anything that would embarrass the University of Texas or Rice University. However, I told the reporter, "I've been relaxed about it for a long time. Sometimes, though, I'd like to wear my tennis shoes all the time. But then, you can't very well sit at a head table in evening clothes and tennis shoes."

97

Chapter 14

Pink Clouds
with Ground-glass Edges

In the spring of 1961, Pat was graduating from high school. She was busy and kept me busy with a round of social activities. I was involved, as always, with many University Ladies Club programs.

One morning I was getting dressed to go to a Ladies Club meeting; I leaned over to put on my bra and noticed a small dimple in the skin of my left breast. I could not feel a lump, so I went ahead and dressed and attended the meeting.

I made an appointment with our family doctor. He examined me and said, "I wouldn't worry about it. It's just a little bit of tissue."

Two weeks later I went to another doctor, who also said he didn't believe it was anything serious. On Friday, at the end of that second week, I had made all the arrangements for a Coke party for Jan Bennett, Pat's dearest friend, who was graduating with Pat. The party was scheduled for Sunday afternoon, two days from then.

That Friday afternoon I had an appointment with Dr. John Thomas, Pat's cancer surgeon. After the examination, I went back into his office. He said to me, "Gene, I think we need to have a biopsy, but I'm convinced it is malignant." I looked straight at him, tried to read more from his face, but it was inscrutable. The lids had dropped halfway to hide the expression in his eyes.

"We'll have to wait another week or two because Pat will be graduating from high school," I answered. "Dr. Thomas, you remember how we feared we'd never see that day. It's an important time for me . . . and, besides, she and I have planned a Coke party for one of her friends Sunday afternoon."

"I think you need to go into the hospital as soon as the last girl has drunk the last Coke," he said. "If you wait to see Pat graduate, you will never see any of your other children graduate. "Get Norman to bring you to the hospital by 6:00 in the evening on Sunday. We'll do the biopsy early Monday morning."

"Okay," I answered.

*   *   *

Just as Dr. Thomas had ordered, I checked into the hospital Sunday evening and had all the tests and preparation for surgery. Dr. Thomas came by that evening just to touch base, and said the surgery would be early the next morning. He would do the biopsy; if the result was a malignancy, he would go ahead and do the surgery right then.

I don't remember that night, if I slept or not, or being wheeled into surgery. The next thing I remember was John Thomas' face leaning over me. He looked like a serious turtle, with his eyes slitted, half closed, again inscrutable.

"It was cancer," he said, "but we've got it all."

At that point someone jabbed a needle into my hip, and I remember nothing more until the next morning when Norm came in and said, "Hello." After a pause, he added, "You are going to be all right." Then he said, "You look just like a boy." I wanted to kill him. I started to cry and couldn't stop.

Some person in a white uniform came and gave me a shot in the hip. Even with the shots, which I learned later was morphine, I still had intense pain.

The next day when Norm came into the hospital room, he had important news. "They want me to be vice-president and provost of the university," he said.

I was still floating on a large pink cloud of morphine, edged with ground glass.

"I think I'd rather be a beachcomber," I said.

The ambition in this family was never mine. I thought I had the most wonderful life of all being a full professor's wife. Even through the pink clouds of hidden pain, I think I realized at that

99

moment that our lives would never be the same. What the 1960s and all that decade came to mean for me personally began that day in Seton Hospital. They would be days of pain, days of joy.

*   *   *

In 1961, mastectomies were what they called "radical procedures." My operation was performed in that manner. When the bandages were changed for the first time that day, the doctor was assisted by the nurse who had befriended me when Pat was having her series of surgeries. She was my private nurse during this hospital stay. A student nurse was also on hand, holding the tray for Dr. Thomas. I saw the student's face when she saw what had been done to my body.

She dropped the tray.

I knew the wound was something very, very terrible, and it was. One-fourth of my body had been cut to the rib bones. The muscles were gone. The tendons and flesh were no more. Not only was the chest muscle cut away, but also the muscles down my left arm. They had been severed from my body, leaving movement of my arm almost impossible. I was to learn later that the lymph system had been destroyed in my left arm, so that any cut or even a bee sting had no plumbing to carry away the infection, and my arm would swell two or three times its size from shoulder to wrist.

The size of my surgical wound was fourteen by ten inches — 140 square inches of weeping area — extending from under my left arm and shoulder throughout the left portion of my chest.

I didn't see it. I was lying on a bed. There was no mirror except the mirror of that student nurse's face.

Several days later, they took the stitches out and put two drains in my side, up under my armpit, toward the back, to drain whatever fluid had to be removed from the wound.

I never saw what I looked like while I was in the hospital. But I felt hurt and angry, betrayed because I hadn't been allowed to help make the decision. I thought Dr. Thomas should have awakened me after the biopsy to discuss what was happening to me before I was so mutilated. With medical knowledge what it was then, the decision would probably have been the same, but at

Pink Clouds with Ground-glass Edges

least I would have been prepared, would have known what to expect. I wanted to be a partner in decisions about my body and my life.

The nurse on duty gave me a bed bath in the mornings. The private nurse was with me two or three nights. Addie Mae was home with the children, so she couldn't be with me. Gradually, however, I didn't need nurses around the clock.

Many friends came by to see me. Norm came every day, and brought the older children — Sally, Steve, and Pat. Katy was only three years old. The hospital didn't allow small children on the floors.

I was still getting frequent bandage changes and daily shots of morphine. People had brought me several books to read. I remember reading nearly all the words of one of them, but didn't know what they were about. I do remember there were wonderful scenes in this book that looked like Arizona mesas with sedimentary streaks — sand, copper, touches of red.

I told a nurse, "I must be losing my mind. I don't remember what I read yesterday or even the name of the book."

She said she could understand because they were still giving me morphine for the almost unbearable pain.

"Your wound is like a big postage stamp that extends under your arm and across your chest — under your skin," she said. "The wound is oozing interiorly. There's nothing under the skin except ribs."

I turned my head away. Emotional pain and physical pain were fighting for my very being as a person.

*　　*　　*

The enormous changes in my life had to do not only with being sick for a period of time, but with the massive changes in my body and my self-image, of lessened immunity to minor ailments like colds and sore throats. All of this was happening at a time when I was being pushed to center stage. Far from being the wife of a chemistry professor, I was now the wife of the vice-president of the university and it was now my duty to stand in university receiving lines, greeting as many as 1,500 faculty members and their wives. I knew that at any time someone would ask the

101

question of me, "Which one was it, Gene?" And I would answer, "You'll never know which one is the Toni."

Friends and strangers alike were curious. One good friend came to see me at home. As we drank coffee, she asked, "Could I see your scars?" Others, the mothers of children in school with mine, and the mothers of my Girl Scouts, felt comfortable asking me this kind of intimate question.

I went to Nan's, where I had previously bought most of my clothes, to find a dress with sleeves that were not too tight or a dress with a self-material belt that I could use to extend the sleeves. I knew the saleswoman quite well, so I tried on many different dresses to find one to accommodate my new needs. The woman who usually waited on me took me into one of the dressing rooms so she could look. I was a curiosity.

I never went back to that shop.

*   *   *

When I went home from the hospital, Addie Mae settled me in the lounge chair on the glassed-in porch. Mr. McCann had installed a pulley from the ceiling directly over the chair to help me do pulling exercises to train the muscles in my lower arm to take over the tasks of the missing muscles.

Pat went to her graduation, but her mother didn't. Later that evening, she went to the senior party, which lasted a long time. I remember Norm getting out of bed several times, looking for Pat and listening for her. Finally, she did come in and told us she and her date had been sitting on the dock at Lake Austin watching the boats and the lights.

That was Friday night. Saturday morning Norm said he was going to Washington.

"Why are you going to Washington on Saturday?" I asked. "There won't be any offices open in Washington until Monday."

"My father and mother are old," he answered, "and I'm going to see them."

My sense of rejection was overwhelming.

102

Chapter 15

Keeping On Keeping On

The cancer operation was a devastating experience partly because it happened so quickly. I had no time to prepare for it, no knowledge of what it would be like, and no premonition of its aftershocks.

After I went home to Sharon Lane, the long slow healing began. My life would never be the same again — and this was not entirely because of the operation. As I've written, Norm was appointed vice-president of the University of Texas at Austin in 1961. Two years later Dr. Joseph Smiley, the university president, abruptly resigned to accept the presidency at the University of Colorado. It was widely rumored and also reported in the press that Norm would be the new president of the University's Main Campus in Austin. However, this was not to be for five more years. Instead the Regents incomprehensibly restructured the University System organization, leaving the Main Campus presidency vacant, and giving Norm the title of vice-chancellor for academic affairs, with the budgetary, administrative, and academic duties of a large university's chief executive officer.

Whatever Norm was called in the university hierarchy, we as a family were thrust into the public eye. The world I went back to after I left Seton Hospital was considerably different from the one I had left just ten days before. Gradually my strength returned, and I diligently did the prescribed exercises to retrain my arm muscles. My left arm had gone on permanent strike; it no longer obeyed orders.

My psychological balance was good and became better and

103

better as I reflected on my joy in being alive. I thought a lot about what had happened and was happening to me. Those of us who have always read everything we could get our hands on know of atrocities done to women through the ages, including the physical mutilation and dismemberment of women's breasts in Nazi concentration camps, and the psychological mutilation of women, such as that which was visited on those women who were paraded through the streets of Paris naked and with heads shaved during the French Revolution. Intentional or not, breast surgery and chemotherapy, which often causes temporary baldness, are powerful metaphors of violence against women.

In our culture, breasts are powerful symbols of feminine sexuality, as is luxuriant, flowing hair. I found it painful to watch television ads day after day emphasizing these symbols of beauty and feminine identity, at a time when I was weakened and vulnerable, and striving to put my life back together.

I was appalled by the word "mutilation." From the Latin root, mutilar, the word means to cut or lop off, to render imperfect — not the kind of image a woman wants for herself. I am not surprised when some women say they don't want to go on living after this kind of surgery.

This, however, is one of the steps in healing — going through a period of hopelessness, then joy in being alive, and finally coming to realize that being a woman and all that beautiful word entails does not have to end. We must all wrestle with our grief for the loss of a breast, but we do grow out of it eventually. And when we do, it's a great triumph. Most of us feel stronger for it.

So many times since 1961 I have visited women who have had mastectomies, and I have longed to be able to help them through the stages of pain and sorrow. But nobody can do it for another. One has to do it herself. No talk will enable a person to accept this horrendous event; each woman has to do it alone.

If a cancer patient loses hair during chemotherapy treatment, the consolation is that it will grow back, thicker and more beautiful than before. And you will still be alive. Many quite satisfactory prostheses are now on the market to be worn in a pocket in your own bra.

While some mastectomy patients say they do want to die,

most are joyous for the chance to live. The most devastating experience of all is the fear that you are going to die. When I went to my doctor's office for a checkup after the surgery, he asked how I felt.

"I'm feeling very good," I answered.

Then he said, "You aren't out of the woods yet." Then he mentioned the odds — thirty to seventy percent survival rate. "If you live as long as fifteen months, then you have a chance of staying alive longer."

During those months of healing, I continued my private and numerous conversations with God. "If I am going to die," I told Him, "I need to make some changes in my life." And so I did.

People who have known me only casually, in a public way, shaking hands in a receiving line, seeing our family's pictures in newspapers, living a public life, do not know that I am and always have been innately shy. My shyness was most obvious in my inability to tell my friends how much they meant to me, how much I cared about them.

So I made some changes here. Instead of saying to a friend, "That's a pretty dress," I changed the compliment to "*You* look pretty in that dress."

It took me even longer to stumble over my shyness to say, "I love you," to my friends. Gradually, however, it became a way of life, and I have reaped enormous rewards. To cherish is to be cherished.

From that day in 1961, when I went home to Sharon Lane, until this very day, I have beside my bed a book called *The Healing Light*. The author's wonderful understanding of how to be in touch with God, even in mundane things, and her gift of putting this into words, helped me to get in touch and keep in touch with God. I find the book so helpful that over the years I have bought dozens of paperback editions to give to other cancer patients, if they care to have them.

I believe that God does heal, and that in conjunction with the medical skills of doctors, He does not fail us.

*   *   *

In addition to the awesome task of patiently learning and

105

watching as our physical wounds heal, all of us in this sisterhood of breast cancer are gripped with fear. First, we are fearful of the operation itself, then of the pain following. As we begin our physical healing, we are now truly vulnerable. We know the statistical chances of our living one year, five years, a normal life span. And we know women who are (or were) those statistics — friends who have died.

Fear can tear us apart or it can make our lives more precious, more intense. Life can be so beautiful that we strive to live it fully one day at a time.

Many times in the very beginning we all feel guilty, questioning, "What did I do to deserve this?" or "I must be a very bad person to have such a terrible thing happen to me."

But cancer doesn't come as punishment. Knowledge in its creeping and slow way is shedding some light on causes of cancer — environmental, nutritional, inherited predisposition. Even so, cancer's causes in individual instances remain elusive, but we do know it is *not* caused by our own "badness."

We have no guilt to assume.

Fear we do have. I have come to believe that being afraid is not weakness, and that sickness is not of our own doing. It is weakness, however, to wallow in either sickness or fear. We must be about the business of healing. For women, one of the first steps toward wellness and a new wholeness is care for our physical appearance. Some may call this vanity; I call it good sense. It's essential for ourselves, our families, our dearest friends, and even for strangers, that we look as good as we can.

If we can show a whole-looking figure to the world, using artificial aids and care in selecting clothes that are becoming and well-fit, we are on our way.

Soon after I had settled back into being at home with the children and Norm, I — with Addie Mae's help — made an inventory of my wardrobe. What did I have that I could wear now? Not very much. Out were the low-necked dresses. Out were the sleeveless garments. Out were the tight sleeves. My left arm would be forever swollen, some days worse than others. Useless were the dresses that had to be pulled over my head and those that buttoned in the back because I couldn't use my left shoulder. Try

106

putting on a dress being able to raise only one arm! I no longer could tie the sashes of dresses or aprons because my left arm would not move toward the back. I couldn't take a lid off a jar because I had no chest muscles. But along the way in this process of healing I learned to deal with these terrible frustrations.

I called Scarbrough's Foundations Department and asked if they carried bras for mastectomy patients. "Yes," was the answer, so I made an appointment and went downtown to look at them. These were regular bras, conventionally sized, but with one pocket in each cup for inserting appropriate prosthesis.

One of the first inserts that I tried was a small plastic bag that I could blow up like a balloon. It was elliptical and outfitted with a short tube to be used to inflate it. This was designed so the bosom size could be adjusted to what was right for each individual. This was fairly satisfactory, but I was very nervous when I was scheduled to stand in receiving lines — a frequent occurrence — and I saw a young woman approaching me with a corsage and pin!

Another hazard I discovered with this device was altitude. When I went out to New Mexico to pick up Sally from camp at Cloud Croft, I drove many thousands of feet into the mountains. The higher I went, the larger my left bra cup swelled. Disconcerting to say the least!

Most of us do not have unlimited funds to buy whole new wardrobes, so we have to remake what we have. As I began the rehabilitation of my clothes, it became a creative challenge.

Since I had originally purchased most of my clothes at Nan's, I asked the buyer to get in touch with the manufacturers and ask if they had any more fabric like that used in the dresses I wanted to have altered. I was grateful, too, for generous facings and for belts made of the same material as the dresses. The facing material used in suit lapels was a bonanza for this kind of wardrobe restructuring. An expert seamstress could enlarge sleeves using this material, then redo the lapels using a lining material. Another often-used garment renovation was the change of back openings to side or front. I couldn't lift my arm to get a dress or blouse over my head, but side openings gave me room to maneuver.

Knit garments stretched to accommodate an arm that swelled and then went down from time to time. I started acquiring knit clothes and gradually have assembled a practical wardrobe. As I added a new dress or suit to my wardrobe season by season, I gradually increased the number of my clothes that open down the front. My wardrobe runs toward knit suits and classic shirtwaist dresses. Fortunately, these clothes stay in style year after year.

Another help was the strategically placed black bow. If a V-necked garment plunged too low, I pinned a bow at the cleavage point to camouflage the area.

These efforts at clothing reconstruction worked so well for me that I wrote an article for any woman who has had a mastectomy, describing how to remake a pre-operation wardrobe. I spent hundreds of hours drawing sketches and writing precise directions. This article was published in the *Vogue Pattern Magazine.*

As I recovered, my intense sympathy for other women with breast cancer became a way of life. When a friend, an acquaintance, or even a friend of a friend had this surgery, I made it a point to visit her in the hospital, taking my little packet of small gifts — a rope to put over a shower curtain rod to exercise damaged muscles and to regain strength in the arms, notations about exercises such as "climbing the wall with one's fingers" to train an arm to lift itself again, and, of course, Agnes Sanford's *The Healing Light.* I also brought the gift of myself, the support and example of an ordinary woman who had survived the pain and fear the other woman was going through at that moment.

I continued to be disturbed that women undergoing breast surgery were not being told what to expect and were mostly left out of decision-making about their own bodies. Although I had little chemotherapy, I was also troubled by the added indignity that often accompanied it — the loss of hair, the nausea.

Dr. Robert Morton at M.D. Anderson Hospital invited me to Houston to talk with the doctors there about some of these concerns. I told them what I would have liked to know about my own surgery and treatment, and I listened to their side. It did turn out to be at least a two-sided issue. Some of these wonderful doctors truly believed that if women knew what to expect, they would hesitate to undergo the operation. One even said, "Some women, if they knew, would run down the hall screaming and never come back," refusing the opportunity to live and return to health. I disagreed and still do. I believe that knowledge is power, and that the more one knows, the better one can prepare for what is to come.

These sessions at M.D. Anderson resulted in my receiving an invitation from Princeton University to participate in a seminar of physicians and others involved in cancer research — both medical and psychological aspects.

I had written the paper, had airline reservations and was looking forward to the trip when I found a small lump in my right breast.

"I'm entering the hospital for a post-graduate course," I wired the Princeton people.

Chapter 16

Autographs and Yucca

For the Hackerman family, the 1960s began not with Norm becoming vice-president of the university of Texas, not with my cancer. For us, as for millions of others, the sixties began with the young American president's ringing inaugural challenge: "Ask not what your country can do for you, but what you can do for your country."

Norm and I were at the Capitol in Washington on the snowy January day when John F. Kennedy was inaugurated as president of the United States. We stayed with Norm's sister, Rita, and her husband, Joe Lieberman, in Bethesda.

Our seats were on the steps of the House of Representatives' side of the Capitol. My mind was running eighty miles per minute thinking about the enormity of it all: two citizens, one a first-generation American and the other, a child of people who had come to these shores fifteen generations ago, sitting together, feeling the same emotions, the same pride and love of country. The words of the president, my own overwhelming emotions, and the cold of the day did bring on one of my migraines, perhaps to make that day even more indelible.

The 1961 inaugural was the beginning of what would become for us a close acquaintance with the White House. Lyndon Johnson was, of course, sworn in as vice-president that same day, and we, as Texans, had been invited by him to attend the inauguration.

After November 22, 1963, the LBJ Ranch at Stonewell, Texas, became the vacation White House, with Austin the crossroads between Washington and the Ranch. Often, Norm was included in White House social events that involved scientific personalities. Remember — many have forgotten — that Lyndon Johnson was an avid proponent of space exploration, and he truly was the "Education President," believing as he did that education was the way out of poverty and powerlessness.

Norm was in Lyndon Johnson's Oval Office when Norm's appointment to the Board of the National Science Foundation was announced. Later, Norm's colleagues on the Board would elect him chairman. He filled the Foundation chair longer than any other scientist — nearly a decade — and served on the Board by appointment of three U.S. presidents. Norm carried this responsibility at the same time he was president of Rice University. Every week through Thursday, Norm was on the Rice campus. Then he took an evening plane to Washington to spend Thursday evening, Friday, Saturday, and Sunday working on the materials left for his attention at the Foundation. He arrived back in Houston on the late plane from Washington on Sunday night. These made for lonely weekends for me, but I felt, as did Norm, that this work was important and worth the sacrifice.

We were invited to several formal functions at the White House. Trips to the LBJ Ranch were frequent and always stimulating and enjoyable. Mrs. Johnson was an impeccable hostess, paying attention to every guest's interests. Since most of the guests were from distant places and thus invited only once, the format of the ranch parties was much the same. Barbeque was the usual fare, with tables set up on the splendid greensward, which rolled uninterrupted from the Ranch House itself to the Pedernales River. Entertainment ran toward the Geezenslaw Brothers, with their distinctive country music and humor. Other entertainers were precision ropers and whipsnappers, who could flick a cigarette out of the mouth of a colleague at twenty paces, giving Yankee guests a touch of the Old West. Cactus Pryor, whose one-liner timing rivaled Bob Hope's, was the dependable emcee.

One party that stands out in my mind was on June 2, 1968 — still wildflower time in the Hill Country. It was toward the end of the Johnson era, while the LBJ Library was being planned for the University of Texas. Many of the guests were donors to the library.

The Time Has Come

Our invitation came by telephone. Mrs. Johnson called me at the UT President's House to invite us.

"It will be informal," said Mrs. Johnson. "Just wear old clothes. We have some interesting guests, and I want you to see the wildflowers."

In those days, we had a little blue Volkswagen. I'll never forget our dashing arrival at the LBJ Ranch House. We were late. What seemed like a large group of people was assembled on the porch, apparently waiting for us.

Over on the launching pad, two helicopters were warming up. One was a large 'copter, with room for twenty passengers, and the other was small, holding only four. The small one had a glass bubble so passengers could watch the ground.

Norm was directed to the large helicopter. Bess Abel, Mrs. Johnson's assistant, said to me, "I know how much you like the wildflowers, so I saved a seat for you in the bubble."

Bess and I scurried out to the small whirly-bird, and she said, "Climb in the back, and I'll sit with the pilot." There was one other passenger already in the back.

After the confusion of boarding and getting settled, I turned to the person on my left, and said, "I'm Gene Hackerman."

"I'm Gregory Peck," the gentleman answered.

Holy Cow! Gregory Peck, my very favorite movie personality of all time! (Only once during the day did I really act like a star-struck teenager. But I'll tell about that later.)

I finally got my mouth closed, my jaw back in place, and uttered a few intelligent words.

It so happened that I had seen all of Gregory Peck's movies. *David and Bathsheba, The Designing Woman, To Kill a Mockingbird.* All of them. Also, I knew he had been at the university speaking to drama classes, so we had much to talk about.

We landed at the Krim Ranch, about thirty minutes from the LBJ Ranch. The Krim Ranch belonged to Mr. and Mrs. Arthur Krim. I learned he was a motion picture executive and a lawyer and special counsel to President Johnson.

The schedule was for the guests to go by automobile to the nearby lake for a boat ride before lunch at the Krims. This was a short ride, so the same cars were shuttling the guests to the Boat

112

House. Mrs. Johnson was taking the last car, and she suggested that she and I take "a little walk, down through the wildflowers." We did, and I don't remember a more spectacular display — dazzling with color in the summer sunshine.

When we returned from our walk, Mrs. Johnson invited me to ride with her in a Secret Service car. Mrs. Johnson sat in front with the Secret Service man, and I climbed into the back seat, where one passenger was already seated. I turned to him and said, "I'm Gene Hackerman."

"I'm Henry Ford," he said, and indeed he was. He and his wife, the famous beauty, Cristina Vettore Austin, had been weekend guests at the Johnsons' Ranch. Cristina had gone ahead in the president's car.

When we arrived at the lake, we again had a choice of conveyances — a large boat or a smaller speedboat with LBJ at the helm. Having ridden with him in cars, which he drove at the speed of A. J. Foyt, I politely declined riding in the smaller boat. In the big boat, I sat down by a woman from California, Mrs. Lew Wasserman. Her husband was head of the Music Corporation of America (MCA). We exchanged pleasantries, and began a rewarding conversation. She told me that she had recently had a mastectomy and still wasn't feeling up to par. I told her of my own experience, and during the remainder of the boat trip, we formed a warm bond. I mentioned that our daughter lived in Los Angeles and that I often visited there.

She invited me to visit her in Beverly Hills the next time I was there. She gave me her card and phone number. Shortly thereafter, on a trip to Los Angeles to visit Pat and her family, I spent a pleasant afternoon with Mrs. Wasserman at her Beverly Hills home, after lunching at the Bistro.

After the boat ride, we returned to the Krim Ranch, where a barbeque lunch was waiting. There I was able to visit with the others guests, including Dr. and Mrs. Robert Benjamin, Mr. and Mrs. Horace Busby, Mr. and Mrs. Edwin Weisl, Sr., Mr. and Mrs. Abraham Feinberg, and Frank Erwin.

I rode in the big helicopter on the way back to the LBJ Ranch. When we arrived at the airstrip, cars were waiting to take us to the house. The president was at the wheel of a big white Lincoln convertible, with a Secret Service car and two agents following. That following car contained a fully stocked bar, and ever so often we stopped and the agents carried drinks to the presidential car.

"Come on, Gene, you and Norm get in with us," the president invited. We did. In the front seat with LBJ was the gorgeous Cristina Ford. The president was at his most dashing, most courtly. He drove, not on the road, but through the fields of wildflowers. They were tall as the tops of the doors, reaching high up the sides of the car. We could reach out of the convertible and touch them.

We came to the gate. Beside it was a spectacular blooming yucca plant. LBJ jumped out of the car to open the gate. He cut off two branches of the yucca, and gave one to Cristina and one to me.

Velvet-nosed deer, tame as bottle-fed lambs, came up to the car, and LBJ slowed down to feed them cigarettes from the palm of his hand.

Mrs. Johnson had a little snack ready when we arrived at the Ranch House. This was the last event of the day for us and the last of the weekend for the Johnsons' house guests. It was at this supper that I committed what I suppose was a *faux pas,* but I'm glad I did it.

"Could I have your autograph?" I asked Gregory Peck. Somebody produced a piece of paper, and Mr. Peck wrote his name. The president, observing this, came over and asked plaintively, "Gene, don't you want *my* autograph, too?"

"Of course, Mr. President," I answered. President Johnson signed *three* autographs on separate slips, the extra ones for my children.

Then began the president's personal ferrying by automobile of the departing guests to the runway. Leaving aboard the Ford plane were the Fords and the Wassermans. The next trip took Mr. and Mrs. Krim, the Weisls, the Feinbergs, and the Benjamins to the Krim plane.

The Gregory Pecks departed by car to catch a commercial flight to California. A few minutes later, Norm and I boarded our little blue Volkswagen and whirled away toward Austin with a stick of yucca and a handful of autographs.

Chapter 17

Tilting at Windmills

hile the children were little, most of my community work circled around the Girl and Boy Scouts,
the Parent-Teacher Association, and the University Ladies Club. I enjoyed all of these activities,
poured myself into them, and made lifelong friends. Looking
back, I realize all of these activities were fulfilling my sense of
responsibility to the city and community in which we lived, even
as they provided an outlet for my creative and social urges.

And most of these activities were directly involved with children. To be frank, I have always preferred small people to the big
people — and so it was then.

My developing sense of responsibility to the community
came during what I call my "growing up period" in the 1960s,
when I served three terms on the Travis County Grand Jury, and
learned about another side of Austin, one that had been, until
then, largely hidden from me. It was my introduction to man's
inhumanity to man.

A grand juror is nominated for service by a county official.
Grand juries differ from petit juries in that they do not decide the
guilt of a particular person in a particular case. Our job, over the
three-month period of a grand jury's service, was to decide
whether a crime had indeed been committed and whether there
was justification for an indictment that would bind the accused
over for a trial.

The grand juries on which I served met five days a week,
starting at noon and continuing all day. We usually went home

115

around 7:00 in the evening, but there were times when we worked through the evening, and even up until midnight if there were a number of cases to be heard.

The cases before the Travis County Grand Jury were heard in categories; that is, we heard all bad check cases on one day and all burglary cases on another. The reason for categorizing the cases we heard was to keep different sections of the police department from being tied up working with us every day.

I learned a new vocabulary. "Paperhanging" had nothing to do with decorating a room. It was the term used for bad-check writing. A "paperhanger" wrote bad paper, then hung it on someone else.

The procedure was the same each day, whether long or short. The day began with the affable and legendary Rudy Cisneros dropping by to bring us doughnuts from his Cisco's Bakery, an East Austin gathering place for politicians and newspeople.

The district attorney came to the jury room to present the case he had. Witnesses were called, with the first set of witnesses being the policemen involved, usually the arresting officer.

Late in the week — Thursday or Friday — we heard the capital crimes. These hearings often went on well into the night. It was while hearing about these capital crimes that I began suffering with horrible migraine headaches. I couldn't believe the things people did to each other.

On one grand jury, we listened to a case about a child molester. This was particularly difficult for me, as I thought about my own daughters and how I would feel if one of them had been the victim.

As the only woman on this particular grand jury, I was asked by the chairman to question the little girl. That was probably the hardest thing I ever had to do on the jury. I thought about my questions a lot, and how I could gently question the child about what had been done to her without adding to her trauma. After that day was over, I was absolutely wiped out. As soon as I got home, I called my wise sociologist friend Dr. Bernice "Bunk" Moore of the Hogg Foundation. I went over what had happened that day and asked her opinion of what I had said and done.

116

Tilting at Windmills

"Do you think I did more harm?" I asked Bunk. "No," she answered. "You did just right." And so I was able to sleep.

Again, unlike a petit jury, the grand jury hears all the evidence, including all the previous crimes committed by the accused. Jury members will take into consideration the fact that a seventeen-year-old boy before them has been stealing since he was ten.

When the accused was young, I was more prone than the men on the jury to suggest, "Let's give him a chance. Let's talk to him when he comes in . . . perhaps he will understand better that he shouldn't do such things." I was often convinced that many of these kids were committing crimes because they simply didn't know better.

My first cancer operation occurred in the middle of my first grand jury. I was in the hospital several weeks. I remember a "get well" card from my colleagues with a note in it: "Hurry up and get back. All these juveniles need you!"

My "bleeding heart" for some of these kids was justified. Some were ignorant of what is and is not a crime. One case I remember quite well involved a young man seventeen or eighteen years old, a member of the Longhorn Band. Riding his motorcycle, he had picked up his band uniform from the cleaners. He was carrying it over his shoulder as he rode down North Lamar Boulevard toward the university. A car full of teenagers went by, slowed, and one of the boys rolled down his window. He grabbed the uniform, and the car sped off. They had stolen a seventy-five-dollar uniform. (Stealing anything worth more than fifty dollars was a crime larger than a misdemeanor.) Not only was the uniform-snatcher charged, but also his companions.

Obviously, I voted to no-bill these boys. But my own children that night heard a lot of "Don't you evers . . ."

Another time we encountered a fresh-faced young Navy ROTC man. His crime had to do with falling in love. He was crazy about this girl and wanted to buy her an engagement ring. He had written a check on his roommate's account and presented it at the jewelry store.

Now, the roommate would have forgiven him and let him

117

pay the money back. The bank, however, caught the check and realized that the signature was not the account holder's signature. It was the bank that had brought the matter to the attention of the district attorney. The boy's parents were devastated. Need I say that I was the one who voted out in left field?

Another memorable case involved a young black man who accompanied his cousin to the Capital National Bank on Seventh Street. At the time, all the banks had counter checks. (That was before the days of account numbers.) His cousin, who had an account at the bank, wrote a counter check and withdrew some money. The next day the young man returned to the bank, this time without his cousin, wrote a fifty-dollar counter check, and signed his cousin's name.

The lad cashed the check, then walked down Sixth Street, where he bought a pair of shoes and had some lunch. He then returned to the bank and deposited the money left over from the fifty dollars into his cousin's account. That's when the bank teller called the police. I still believe this was more naiveté than criminality.

I think we all sometimes forget how much we need to know to live in America today, just to do the routine things that come up every day. I found that many charged with hot check writing simply didn't know it was wrong to write checks if the money wasn't in the bank. A lot of truth hides in the stories of children who want something, and when told by their parents, "We don't have the money," suggest, "You have some checks, don't you?"

Sometimes I could persuade my colleagues to give people a second chance, but not often when they had had previous difficulties with the law.

While I was serving on one grand jury, Rock Hudson was at the University of Texas, lecturing to drama classes and working with student actors.

The day Rock Hudson appeared before our grand jury was a day to remember. This gorgeous hunk of man with his winning smile and gracious manner was actually sitting at the table just a few feet from me. We had heard testimony from his manager that he had asked the manager to procure a boy for him. Rock Hudson admitted that this was so. Working with the district attorney, we jurors decided to suggest to Hudson that he leave Austin immediately and pledge never to come back.

Looking back, I think this was a good decision.

I tried to turn down another opportunity to serve on the grand jury after Norm was named president of the university. I treasure a remark made by then District Judge Mace Thurman: "Mrs. Hackerman, the grand jury needs you worse than the University of Texas does."

I enjoyed and learned from the grand jury experience. It fit into my ideals of civic conscience, and into the reason I like so much the print of Picasso's "Don Quixote" hanging on the wall outside my office. It was my opportunity to tilt at some new windmills!

Chapter 18

Grandchildren

As I've said, since my mother died when I was a baby, I had no role model for mothering. I had to learn to be a mother, my occasionally confused efforts urged on by love and pride, trying hard for just the right measure of indulgence and discipline. And yet while I didn't know how to be a mother when I took the job, I suppose I have always known how to be a grandmother. For this job, I had the best model in the world. I lived with my grandmother in Baltimore from the time I was twelve through high school. Nearly three-score years later, I still catch myself nearly every day repeating something that Grandmother said.

She urged that one should make the best of whatever she had. She said it this way: "If you have a shoe with a hole in the toe, and your toe sticks out, polish the toe along with the shoe."

She was a neat housekeeper, and so am I. "A place for everything and everything in its place" was her axiom for household orderliness. Another related saying was, "If you don't take care of the little things that need repair, you never can fix the big things."

Grandmother liked to tell the story of the lost nail: "For the lack of a nail, a shoe was lost, for the loss of a shoe, the horse was lost . . ."

A Golden Rule person, she believed we ought to treat others as we wish to be treated ourselves. Grandmother often told me, "You can catch more flies with honey than with vinegar."

My family teases me because I dress for the day when I get

Grandchildren

up — with hose, hair arranged, jewelry . . . whatever is called for during the morning. But I know no other way to do it. I never saw my grandmother lolling about. She had a great deal of pride in her appearance, and dressed to go to the grocery store as if she might run into the First Lady.

This is not to say that Grandmother was overdressed. Never. But she always dressed in daytime, putting on corset, stockings and shoes. I remember particularly her wearing what she called "Hoover aprons." These were nice cotton wraparound dresses that had narrow sashes that pulled through holes under the arms and tied in the back. My favorites were one of royal blue, with three-quarter length sleeves, white collar and cuffs, and another of a kind of muted gray/pink shade.

Her pride in appearance continued when her hair began to gray. She touched it up with a strong tea rinse.

Perhaps my interest in building and in architecture also came from my grandmother. When the porch needed painting, we painted it. When furniture needed repairing, we got out the tools and screws and made a table leg secure or stripped and refinished a damaged table top. No task deterred her. My grandmother's optimism never wavered.

As the Great Depression closed in around us, just as it did all of America, she cut more corners to take care of herself and me. She sewed "for the public," as we used to say. I recall a continuous stream of ladies coming to be fitted and talking over their wardrobe plans with my grandmother. I can remember going to sleep many a night hearing the whir of Grandmother's sewing machine.

So I knew about grandmothering when Wendy was born. She was my first grandchild, and Pat's first baby. I went to California for Wendy's birth and stayed almost a month. When I came home, Addie Mae flew to Los Angeles to stay a few weeks more with Pat and Wendy. Petite and beautiful, Wendy seemed to me a miracle — and she still does. We are unashamed in our admiration for each other. When she's around, I like to just sit and stare at her. At Norm's and my fiftieth anniversary party, Wendy took just one look at the flowers, the table arrangements, and in an excited voice said, "Grandma, you did good!" And it

121

The Time Has Come

was one of the greatest compliments of the night, right up there with Norm's toast to "my wife of fifty years and my friend for fifty-five."

One has to keep some decorum and modesty in bragging about one's own children, but those rules don't apply for grandchildren. We can be unashamedly proud of them. And so I am of Wendy. When Norm and I, with Neils and Wanda Thompson, went to Los Angeles to a University of Texas–Southern California football game, Wendy was about six months old, and already saying words. When she was five years old, Wendy went with me to Lakeway to get the house ready for her parents and aunts and uncles, who would soon arrive for the holidays. I gave her some picture books to look at while I worked. One of the books was *A Child's Picasso*. She grabbed the book and said, "Oh, Picasso!" I have no idea where she came to recognize Picasso – whether it was from television, or perhaps an excursion Pat took with her to a museum, but I still think it's downright exciting for a five-year-old to be that aware and sensitive.

My children say they always enjoy telling me there's going to be another baby. They know they will hear no moaning about responsibility and how can we make time for yet another. No, the children know that I welcome each new baby with great joy and look forward to the nice person each will become.

And so it was with Pat and Ray's second child. I flew out to California with my daughter, Katy, who was eight years old. Wendy was three, and I wanted to get there early so I could take care of her while Pat was in the hospital.

The day after I arrived Pat drove the four of us to Beverly Hills to see her doctor. After her examination, we all went to the drug store in the same building for a soda. As we sat drinking Cokes, Pat's water broke. I called the doctor upstairs, and he said, "Take her to the hospital."

I drove Pat's car, which I'd never driven before, with a mother in labor sitting beside me, and two small children sitting behind me – one saying, "What's the matter with Mommy? Why is Mommy crying?" (that was Wendy), and the other saying, "What's the matter with Pat? Why is she groaning?" (that was eight-year-old Katy). I'd never driven in that city before, and Pat,

122

between groans, was trying to give me directions to a hospital I'd never been to before. Ray met us at the hospital, and the baby was born. I saw the baby, beautiful like Wendy. We went back to Pat and Ray's home . . . happy, all going well. I had seen Pat, and she was radiant, like Christmas morning.

Ray stayed at the hospital, but came home for dinner. He suggested he would stay with the children so that I could go back to the hospital for another visit. I said, "No, Pat will want you there. I saw the baby this afternoon, so I'll stay here." Ray ate his supper and left for the hospital.

I was reading to the children when the phone rang. It was Ray, incoherent. I finally made out what he was saying, "The baby's dead. The baby's dead." I couldn't make any sense of what he was saying. He rang off.

I called Pat's friend who lived across the street. She came to watch the children, and I went to the hospital. There I pieced together what had happened. The baby had been fine when she was dressed and placed in the bassinet in the hospital nursery. Sometime later the baby vomited, unnoticed by the nursery staff, and choked to death. The needlessness of the tragedy was over-whelming. I kept thinking of Anne Morrow Lindbergh's book, *Days of Gold, Days of Lead.* How soon a golden day can turn lead-en, without warning, without reason.

Pat's doctor administered sedatives to both Pat and Ray. They lay together in the hospital room, she in her bed of pain and he on a cot, sleeping. Every few minutes one of them sobbed. Their pain cut through sleep, through sedation. I sat in a chair watching over them all night.

I remembered when Pat was a child how I would fix her bro-ken baby dolls for her — sew on new hair, get the doll people to put eyes back in. But I couldn't fix this baby. This wasn't the kind of hurt a mother can kiss and make well.

Katy and I stayed about ten more days. During that time I tried to make things right, but, of course, I never could. I did things like have the baby's crib removed before Pat got home from the hospital and arranged for a housekeeper for two weeks after I left. I paid the housekeeper in advance, so Pat wouldn't have to worry about that.

123

The Time Has Come

Another thing I did I hope was helpful, although to this day I wonder. When the mail came the day Pat came home, it included an envelope from the hospital containing a picture of the baby lying beside Pat on the hospital bed the day she was born. Seeing the picture tore me apart, and I didn't know what it would do to Pat.

So I gave it to Pat's brother-in-law, who was also a doctor and lived close by. I asked him to give it to Pat when she was a little better. I don't know, I really don't know. I hope I did the right thing.

After Pat got home, Katy and I flew back to Texas. When we got off the plane in Austin, Steve and Mary were there to meet us. As we walked to the car, Steve said, "Mama, we are going to have a baby." God in His infinite wisdom always provides for us to have joy along with sorrow.

The Lord giveth, and the Lord taketh away.

Chapter 19

Malibu

The French novelist Georges Simenon once said that he could never truly know a woman until he had been her lover. I sometimes think I can never truly know a place, a part of the country, until we own a house there, until I can scatter some books about, hang some pictures on the wall, drink in the scenes from the windows, and make it truly a Hackerman place. I haven't known as many houses as Simenon knew women, but we have been able to take a part of many places with us always.

This longing for complete immersion in a house is different from acquisitiveness. When we sold Sharon Lane to begin two decades of living in other people's houses — public houses of the University of Texas and of Rice University — one of my friends asked, "How can you bear to part with this house that you built, where the children grew up, where you had so much happiness as well as sorrow?" I was surprised at the question. After all, a house is only bricks or stone, lumber and wallboard. A home one takes with her, in memories and selfhood. While I want to become completely aware of many places, I actually carry home in my heart as a snail carries home on its back.

After Pat and Ray were married, and lived in Los Angeles, we visited them often, and drove around Southern California, drinking in the ocean views and smells, and listening to the sound of the surf and the gentle winds.

Pat knows how I like to look at houses, so that was one of the

125

activities she planned for me — that and shopping at the interesting department stores which the Hollywood stars frequented.

One morning I was sitting on a stone bench waiting for Pat outside of Robinson's, a Los Angeles department store. As I sat there, I realized there was a warmth and friendliness in the air that made me feel at peace. Pat and I had eaten at several wonderful seafood houses on the Pacific and had explored intensively up and down the coast as far as Malibu Cove Colony. As has been so often the case, I did find a house I really wanted, one in Mailbu Cove Colony, a house that could be both a family retreat and a place to entertain friends and Norm's academic associates.

Boris Karloff had a house on three lots in Malibu Cove Colony. Beyond his property was a vacant lot, and next to the vacant lot was the house that would be ours.

When I looked in the front door — through it, that is — I could make out a small front hall, and on the left, a bedroom, with a kitchen to the right, and a stairway about three feet from the entrance. Later, when I was able to go inside, I found an enormous room (30' or 35' x 18') stretching across the house. Right in the center of that space was a fireplace with sliding glass doors on each side. The second floor had two large bedrooms with a connecting bath in between. I immediately felt I was one with it all — with the ocean and the ocean birds, with the sky, the sunsets and sunrises. I had to have this house; I had to *know* it.

Pat and Ray, of course, had seen the house, and Steve, but I didn't know anybody in the area to check it out structurally. Even if I was in love with the house, I didn't want to make a bad investment.

Spike Brennan of San Antonio was a member of the University of Texas Board of Regents. Spike had a friend in the Los Angeles area who was knowledgeable about construction and real estate values. Spike asked him to check the house out for me. He did. Spike called me from San Antonio to tell me the house was in good shape.

So I bought the house — and with it, a moonbeam ladder. At night we turned off the lights inside the house. The moon shining on the water made the Pacific look like a pale beige carpet, and the moon beams seemed to form a ladder for walking up

126

into the sky, to the moon itself. If I'd been a drinker, I might have run out and tried to climb my moonbeam ladder.

Mary and Steve honeymooned in the Malibu house, staying there about a month, and from time to time Norm and I went there with the Brennans or with Wanda and Neils Thompson. Once when the Thompsons were there, Neils and Norm found a rock on the beach — a monstrous rock that looked like an elephant's foot. They carted it up the steps, one man on each side, and placed it in front of the fireplace. When we sold the house, we left the elephant's foot. It had found its permanent home, I trust, in the Malibu house.

Excursions to Malibu were always fun. Even minor disasters seemed to take on a Hollywood kind of laughter, appropriate to Entertainment City. So it was the time Mary Jane Hemperley and I went to California for a weekend. We dressed up for the airplane trip — I wore a white linen suit, which was quite appropriate for a Texas spring, but as it turned out, not for Southern California, which still turned bitter cold at night.

Pat met us at the airplane and took us to the Farmer's Market Motel, where we would stay overnight in a second-floor room. Pat and Ray took us to dinner, introducing us to a wonderful Japanese restaurant Ray had found. We sat on the floor to drink our saki and eat our meal. It was an evening of conviviality — we drank lots of tea, laughed and told jokes. It was one of those memorable times with people with whom you feel completely comfortable.

"Let's go out Doheney Drive," suggested Ray. "It's up over the city and we can see all the lights from the mountains." Both Ray and Pat were proud of their new home, their new city, and wanted to show us all their discoveries, their favorite places.

We got out of the car at one lookout point on Doheney Drive and looked over the city. The wind was whipping at our legs, and ruffling us considerably. But the evening wasn't over yet.

"I want you to have some of the best ice cream in the world," said Ray. He parked in an alley near the ice cream place. As we got out of the car, I said, "I'm freezing." Mary Jane said, "I'm frozen." Just at that moment, *I wet my pants.* Only Mary Jane knew, but we both laughed hysterically.

The Time Has Come

"What's the matter?" asked Pat. "Mama, are you all right?" "Yes," I said, "But we really need to get back to the motel."

On another trip Mary Jane and I borrowed Pat's station wagon, and we drove to Malibu. Pat and her family would be there for dinner the next day. I knew we didn't have logs for the fireplace. As we drove, I noted a feed store with logs for sale. I stopped, and asked if it would be possible to deliver a fourth of a cord by noon the next day. I left the telephone number and address.

The next morning Mary Jane and I leisurely walked on the beach, enjoying the scenery, feeling at one with the heavens and the earth, and looking forward to the evening with Pat.

By noon the wood had not been delivered, so I called to ask about it. The person who answered the telephone had a fantastic story: "We had to deliver a big load of hay up into the hills and we went off the road in the driveway at the horse farm, and the back wheels of the truck went over the cliff. We have been having a dickens of a time getting it back onto the road."

"When do you think we can have the wood?" I asked, trying to stay in control of the conversation.

"Well, I have a few logs in the back of the store," he answered. "If you would like to pick them up . . . I'll put some logs out on the porch of the store tonight."

The weather had turned cold, and we really needed a fire that night, so Mary Jane and I decided we'd follow Pat part of the way back home, and get the logs then.

After dinner we set out, Mary Jane and I following Pat. When we got to the hay and log store, I signaled to Pat to wait in her car while I got out to collect the logs. Mary Jane stayed in the station wagon while I got out to find the logs. No logs were on the porch. I walked around to the back of the store. No logs were there either. Meanwhile, a police car stopped, and the officer got out to check on this prowler around the back of the store — *me!*

"Lady, what are you doing here?" he asked. For some unknown reason, I started to babble: "I was looking for some logs. You see, they delivered some hay up in the hills and the horses were very hungry. They were all out of hay. The truck backed off the cliff, and was just hanging there . . ." I couldn't stop talking, knowing all the time I was making no sense at all. Finally, the police officer stopped me long enough to say, "Lady, just get in your car and go home. Please."

The times when Neils and Wanda Thompson and the Spike Brennans were our guests at Malibu usually were in connection with Longhorn football games. We flew to out-of-town games with the team, and these were happy, convivial occasions. I remember one time landing in Los Angeles with the football team, and we looked out of the airplane window and saw Ray in his Texas Cowboy outfit, with orange chaps and cowboy hat. He was a member of the Texas Cowboys service organization, the one that fires the cannon when the Longhorns score and the one that raises large amounts of money each year for the Texas Association for Retarded Citizens.

Chapter 20

The Sounds of Violence

ugust comprises the dog days, especially in Texas, when the long, hot hours work their power on the souls of human beings. It was on just such a day, a Monday in 1966, when a young man named Charles Whitman went to the top of the University of Texas Tower and began shooting anything that moved. It was later discovered that Whitman had a tiny brain tumor. Indeed, he had told a psychiatrist at the Student Health Center just a few days before that he felt like doing just that, shooting every person in sight from the Tower. But who could believe such a preposterous threat?

It was summertime, and Sally and Katy were at home. The three of us were driving to the Holiday House for a hamburger at noon when we heard on the radio what was happening on the campus.

Neal Spelce's voice on KTBC-Radio invaded the safety of our car.

"This is a warning to the citizens of Austin," said Neal. "Stay away from the university area. Traffic is converging on this area, and there is a sniper on the University Tower firing at will. Several persons have been injured. We have no report on fatalities, but we do know that several have been injured.

"A boy riding a bicycle has been shot and seriously injured. A report of a policeman that has been shot . . . It's like a battle scene.

"There is a shot and another shot. There are two different kinds of shots. Apparently police are returning the fire now.

The Sounds of Violence

Which means there is a danger of ricocheting bullets off the University Tower. We've heard two different reports. One a heavy caliber sounding weapon, apparently a rifle. And another caliber which could be police returning fire. We are not sure that police are returning the fire. But we do hear the shots.

"We now have a report, he is definitely under the clock on the south side. Yes, we can see the movement under the clock of the University Tower. Police are returning the fire."

I began mentally calling the roll of the people I loved most — Sally and Katy were with me. Pat was married and living in California. But Steve was at the university in a class in Garrison Hall — just beneath the Tower! Norm was in the President's Office in the Tower overlooking the South Mall.

"We'll go back to the house and have a sandwich," I told the children. "We have to be there in case Daddy or Steve call."

We waited and waited to hear from Norm and Steve. Then the phone did ring. It was Pat calling from Los Angeles, horrified. She knew Charles Whitman, had had a class with him when she was a student at UT.

"I have to hang up," I told Pat. "I have to have the line free for Daddy or Steve." Not long after that Steve came home to tell me he was all right. The history class in Garrison Hall was just letting out when the shots began. "They told us to get down on the floor," he said. "We could hear the gunshots."

I waited a while longer and called Norm's office. He wasn't there. I spoke with Jim Colvin, vice-president of the university and our good friend.

"Honey, I haven't seen Norm for a while," Jim told me. "He went down on the Mall to help pull wounded people out of the way."

This fanned my anxiety to a fever pitch. I did have a comforting phone call from Orville Wyss, who told me Norm was all right, that he had heard him being interviewed on the radio. But it was very late when Norm, tired and haggard, finally got home.

Charles Whitman's bullets killed sixteen people before his guns were stilled. I did not know until later that evening that Dolly Bolton's grandson, Paul Bolton Sontag, was one of those killed.

Chapter 21

What Hath Violence Wrought?

Norm and I went to Williamsburg, Virginia, the first week in April 1968, to a meeting of the Land Grant Colleges and Universities. This was a treat for me because I could renew old friendships with the people attending, and spend some time exploring Williamsburg as well.

We had not yet moved into the President's House on Meadowbrook, but this was now in the works, though Norm's official title was still vice-chancellor for academic affairs. I had been working for months with Roland Roessner, professor of architecture at the university, remodeling the house, and making it ready for us to move in. Finally the work was done, carpets on the floor and draperies up. However, no furniture had been moved in, neither the new furniture for the public rooms nor our own from Sharon Lane.

I invited the carpenters, painters, plumbers, glaziers, electricians — all the men who had worked on the President's House — and their wives to an open house to view the finished product Easter Sunday, April 7.

We flew into Washington's National Airport, rented a car, and drove to Williamsburg. That night, undressing in our lovely room in the Williamsburg Inn, I noticed a lump in my breast and a sharp pain. I said nothing to Norm about this, but knew I must see Dr. John Thomas as soon as we got back to Austin.

The main banquet of the meeting was Thursday night, April 4. In the middle of dinner, the master of ceremonies stood up and somberly announced that Martin Luther King, Jr., had been shot and killed in Memphis. Because of this terrible, tragic event, the remainder of the meeting was canceled.

The university administrators all scurried about, lining up for phone calls home, revising plane reservations, and standing in groups talking, talking, talking. Everyone had to get home in a hurry, knowing each campus would be in an uproar.

Like the others, Norm was in a hurry to get home, to reach Austin before the Main Campus erupted. The disaffection of students, angered by what they perceived to be the failures of their elders in dealing with Vietnam and racial issues, had moved dozens of campuses to explosion point, though it would be two more years before the worst would come — the incident at Kent State University on May 4, 1970, when nine students were wounded and four killed.

We drove to Washington for the flight back home. As the plane circled the city, I looked out and saw the red flames and smoke rising southwest of the Capitol. Washington was afire, a conflagration set by the sorrow and frustration of grieving and angry people.

All I could think of was "My country 'tis of thee, sweet land of liberty . . ." What have we done to you? What have we done to ourselves?

*   *   *

On our arrival Friday, I called Dr. Thomas. Just as I feared, he ordered me to the hospital for my second cancer operation.

So on that Easter Sunday afternoon, Norm and I hosted the party for the men who had worked on the Meadowbrook House. The refreshment table, bearing punch, coffee and cookies, was set up in the garden. It was a rewarding occasion. One woman told me it was the first time she had seen the artistry of her husband in a job he had talked so much about.

I overheard a cabinet maker showing his wife the remodeled kitchen. "See," he said, "how nice this fits together."

Norm and I posed together for a photograph in front of the house. I was wearing a pink linen dress; it was Easter Sunday.

*   *   *

The Time Has Come

After the party was over, Norm took me to Seton Hospital once again. The next morning my right breast was removed, with the same radical surgery as before, but this time leaving the lymph system and muscles in my right arm. I was in the hospital about ten days.

Before the trip to Williamsburg, I had made drawings of floor plans for each room of the Meadowbrook house, showing where each piece of furniture would go. The furniture had been ordered from Louis Shanks and was ready to be delivered.

Addie Mae and I had discussed which room each of the children would have in the Meadowbrook house. While I was in the hospital, she and my dear friend and neighbor Tinker Morrison supervised the moving of our furniture.

When it came time for me to go home, I left Seton by ambulance and was delivered to the Meadowbrook house, where we would live for the next two years. After that, I never lived in my own house at Sharon Lane again.

Even more than before, I was thrust into the official life of the university. It was commencement time, with all its attendant events and receiving lines.

During the seven years between my cancer operations, Beulah Hodge, a talented television interviewer and producer, and I had worked together writing proposals and sample scripts to get funding for the production of a television film to tell women everything that was then known about breast cancer — how to detect it early, what to expect from surgery, and the few options then open. We had received encouragement from many quarters and the promise of a grant from M.D. Anderson Hospital.

One day, soon after we were settled in the Meadowbrook house, Beulah came by. She had been recovering from breast surgery, and was now up and around. She was radiant and greatly excited. "Oh, Gene," she said, "look at my new breasts." She pulled up her blouse and showed me the results of her preventive surgery and the implants.

Suddenly, if only for a moment, I was envious of Beulah, and angry with her. Of course, it didn't last. More than any other single happening, this innocent occurrence reminded me of how deep was my sense of loss of a very large part of my body.

Chapter 22

A Close Encounter at the White House

N orm and I were invited to spend the night at the White House in late November 1968, during the last weeks of the Johnson presidency. I had watched with admiration and empathy Mrs. Johnson's grace throughout the seven years of both triumph and heartache. I know how hard it must have been to live in the glass bowl of the White House during the 1960s, the fabric of those difficult and turbulent American years rent by the tragedy of Vietnam, the racial unrest in our cities, the terrible assassinations.

Even so, Mrs. Johnson launched beautification programs which continue today, planned her daughters' weddings, realized the joy of her first grandchild. Yes, I feel close to her, although our friendship was mostly formal and ceremonial.

Norm and I had received a telegram on November 8, 1968, inviting us to "an informal reception honoring the National Council on the Arts on Thursday, November 21, 1968, at six o'clock, the White House."

After we accepted this invitation, a call from the White House invited us to spend the night.

*　　*　　*

My earliest recollection of the Johnsons had been the newspaper headlines in connection with the 1948 campaign and Lyndon Johnson's close election to the U.S. Senate. We also

135

knew that the Johnsons had an Austin home on Dillman, not far from our home on Sharon Lane.

While LBJ was majority leader of the Senate, we began seeing the Johnsons at some University of Texas events and other social functions. During this time I worked for Representative Sam Collins in the Texas legislature, and Norm was in the University of Texas administration, thus we were invited to some politically related events in Austin.

At the time I thought of Lyndon Johnson as a towering figure — which he was, at 6'4 (it doesn't seem so tall now that my three grandsons have surpassed that). I remember LBJ's unique handshake. His was not a one-hand shake at all. As he shook your right hand with his, he patted your right shoulder with his left hand, thus giving you a warm, two-handed greeting.

Through Johnson's office, we had received an invitation to the Kennedy-Johnson inaugural events in January 1961. Norm was then vice-president of the university. While LBJ was vice-president, Norm and I went to many events at the LBJ Ranch, always barbeques. There was a method to Lyndon Johnson's madness in his choice of the people around him; he liked to mix academicians with business and political people.

My own feeling, aside from what I have read, is that Mr. Johnson had many anxieties about himself, about his lack of higher education compared to the Harvard degree of John Kennedy. He did everything he could to let people know he was a teacher and interested in education. But I believe his background at Southwest Texas State Teachers College somehow rankled.

Norm was in Washington quite often, working on various scientific assignments, and apparently he was soon considered the White House egghead.

After the Johnsons returned to Texas, Norm and I were invited to a birthday party for Mrs. Johnson at the Headliners Club. Jesse Kellam, manager of KTBC-TV and Radio, and Olga Bredt were also guests. The president offered a toast: "To the Hackermans — Dr. Hackerman is a brilliant educator, and Lady Bird likes him. I like Mrs. Hackerman. There's not another university president's wife who looks like her." Who would not be flattered

136

at such praise? I looked on both of the Johnsons as two people who had done a very good job.

Another memorable occasion attended by the president was the time I lost my petticoat at the head table at a banquet.

The dinner was at the Villa Capri and in honor of Dr. John A. Gronouski, who had been postmaster general in the Johnson Administration and was then dean of the LBJ School of Public Affairs. As I recall, Johnson arrived late at the dinner, sat at the end of the head table, made a few remarks praising his old friend, and left early.

The master of ceremonies introduced the people at the head table, and asked each to stand. I stood up when my name was called. As I rose, I felt the elastic in my petticoat giving way. Uh-oh. As I sat back down, I eased the petticoat over my hips and down around my knees, and soon had the opportunity to pull it completely off. Thank goodness, there was a skirt around the table. But I've often wondered what the waiters thought when they cleaned up and found that petticoat under the table.

One friend suggested my petticoat is probably in some box at the LBJ Library, awaiting the occasion of its display!

*   *   *

But let me return to the night we spent at the White House. We arrived in the afternoon, and our bags were placed in the room we would use. Norm had an appointment at the National Science Foundation. I stayed at the White House. Before Norm left for the NSF, Bess Abel, Mrs. Johnson's social secretary, told us Mrs. Johnson would like us to have tea with her around 3:00. Norm promised to be back in time for this. Bess invited me to go with her below the first level of the White House to watch the rehearsal of the wonderful Alvin Ailey Dancers, who were to perform at that evening's reception.

Later, at the reception, Bess told us that President and Mrs. Johnson wanted us to join them for a late supper in their private quarters. We were the only guests. After supper, Mrs. Johnson excused herself, saying she had to put some finishing touches on a speech she was giving the next day at one of the national forests, where she was planting trees. Norm and I made a move to retire, but the president asked us to stay.

Remember, this was after the election of 1968, after Hubert Humphrey had been defeated by Richard Nixon. The Johnsons were going home to Stonewall, Texas, to retirement and to writing their memoirs.

Norm and I listened to the president as he talked and talked. My impression was that he was still bewildered about what had happened to the country, about Vietnam, and, especially, about the young people.

Over and over he played a videotape of his daughter Luci, and her husband, Pat Nugent, and their little boy, Lyndon. (Luci and Lyndon had met Pat in Hawaii for a few days of rest and recreation.) The president seemed deeply troubled by the young men who had refused to serve their country, and who had decamped to Canada.

I saw a man desperately trying to understand what had gone awry. The only word to describe how I felt is "sad."

Johnson would have been a great president (and he was a great president domestically) had it been an earlier time. I kept thinking of Teddy Roosevelt, and of how well Lyndon Johnson could have filled that role.

Instead, he was thrust into a tragic role, a Lincolnesque role.

That night I couldn't sleep — I kept hearing the caissons of John Kennedy's funeral entourage (remember, this was the fifth anniversary of his death) and of all our other fallen presidents. I thought of King Lear and destiny.

I got up and wrote letters on White House stationery to all my children.

Chapter 23

The President's House at Rice

When Norm accepted the presidency of Rice University, no one had lived in the President's House for several years. Frank Vandiver had been named acting president when Kenneth Pilzer returned to California; the Vandivers had their own home in Houston and did not move. So even though the President's House had been used for student parties and other events, it had not been taken care of as a residence.

When Norm told me he had decided to go to Rice, I was less than enthusiastic. Remember, I was still the person who had arrived in Austin that New Year's Day in 1945, and declared I would never leave. Well, that was twenty-five years before, and apparently, I was going to leave after all.

That spring, I had met the Rice Board of Trustees. A private plane flew to Austin on a Sunday morning to pick us up. We had lunch at the Bayou Club with members of the Board and their wives. It was a pleasant time. I liked them very much. But we returned to Austin that afternoon, without going onto the campus or seeing the President's House.

Then, a few days later, Norm said, "I told Malcolm Lovett and Herb Allen that I'll take that job at Rice."

I *did* need to see that house!

So we went back to Houston. This time, I believe, Sally and Katy and Steve and Mary went along. Very thoughtfully, the Regents had some food — sandwiches and other finger food — laid out on the dining room table for us to eat as we strolled around the house.

The President's House at Rice is a stately building on one of the most beautiful campuses in the world. The campus is a 300-hundred acre academic park shaded by almost 4,000 trees. I liked it at once, but I saw it would need a lot of refurbishing if I were to accomplish what Mr. Lovett had asked of me: to gather people into the President's House — alumni, faculty and students, as well as the Houston community.

"I want you to do for Rice what you did for the University of Texas," Mr. Lovett, chairman of the Board of Governors, told me. "We want to get people to come back to the campus. The behavior of college students all over the country has alienated many supporters of many colleges."

He gave me a free hand. "Make all the changes you want," he said. "We'll hire an architect for you."

We took a walk around the campus and I saw a dozen or so dead birds under the trees. Dead birds? I wondered what had happened.

We went back to the house, and Mr. Lovett gave me a key. No, not to the house, but "the key to Daddy's desk." I felt this was a great compliment and signal of support, since Mr. Lovett's father was Malcolm Odell Lovett, the first president of Rice University. I had the key framed on a bed of blue velvet. When H. Malcolm Lovett, Jr., graduated from Rice, I asked Mrs. Lovett if it would be all right if I gave it to him, and I did.

We had our own furniture for the upstairs family quarters at Rice, but the downstairs areas would need new furniture. I told Mr. Lovett I'd be happy to buy furniture, using my forty percent interior designer's discount, with the provision that when we left Rice I could take what I wanted of the furniture.

"That will be fine," he said.

Fifteen years later Mr. Lovett remembered the conversation, and we brought most of it to Austin with us. I gave Mr. Lovett a copy of all the furniture costs — $6,500 total.

My dreams for the house were that it would be almost like a Williamsburg house, elegant but not ostentatious, a warm, inviting place where many different people could feel comfortable

140

and at home, and yet appreciate that they were in a special house. I wanted it to be conducive to movement and flow, with both inside and outside areas.

I took out the crystal chandeliers, again in the interest of simple elegance. I ordered beautiful hanging brass Williamsburg chandeliers for the dining room and hall. I replaced the fireplace marble with slate, and we used the fireplace for small functions. When the house was full, however, I was afraid someone might back up to the fireplace and catch a jacket or dress on fire.

Nearly every week during the spring and summer of 1970 I went to Houston to work on the house.

The pink brick President's House extended one hundred feet across, a large and inviting house with a circular driveway in the front and a partially covered portico with wrought iron pillars. I immediately realized that a larger roof was needed over the portico to protect guests from the weather. This was built with four square wooden columns supporting the roof. Before parties, when rain was expected, we placed large baskets on both sides of the entry door for umbrellas. A red carpet was installed on the slate porch, running from the step to the door.

Someone asked me, "Why red? Why not Rice blue?"

"I want the red carpet treatment for every guest in this house," I answered.

Another major structural change was the building of a room eighteen by one hundred feet with floor-length windows across the entire back of the house. This considerably enlarged the entertainment area.

A room to the left of the entrance was converted into an office for Norm. This room had dark, heavy paneling. We used a stain remover to take some of the darkness away, then lightly brushed white paint over the wood, creating a striated wood antiqued effect. It was a beautiful room, and Norm spent many hours there, working at his desk and talking with faculty and student visitors.

Continuing the Williamsburg theme, we installed wainscoting in the dining room, with chair rails. Picture moldings were added where walls met ceiling. Faculty artworks were hung from this molding.

The Time Has Come

When I was done with my work, the whole house was white. All the curtains in the house's public rooms were draw draperies, and all the draperies, except the red ones in Norm's study, were off-white. However, certain rooms had draperies of different textures, and were lined with scrim, as were the draperies in Norm's study. The windows across the back had no glass (scrim) curtains. All three of the spaces across the back (the family room, the extension to the dining room, and the long room extending from the living room) had loose, rough, unlined draperies.

In addition to bringing more light into the house via the back windows, I had the dark green walls throughout the house painted my favorite white-with-a-touch-of-gray. The old carpets were taken up and replaced with the off-white carpets I use everywhere.

Elegant simplicity was always the goal. The most utilitarian, economical and striking changes I made were installing the full-size wall mirrors on opposite sides of the dining room, reaching from picture mold to chair rail. These mirrors reflected candlelight and whatever I wished to highlight on the serving tables.

The utility room off the kitchen became my office. Wherever I lived, I have had an office because I have always worked at home, since the days when I typed for Martha Ann Zivley. I covered the sink with plywood and built a door over filing cabinets for a desk. Thus, after we left, the room could easily be converted to a utility room again.

I ordered the furniture through Louis Shanks: white sofas and red and white upholstered chairs (the background was off-white with the *fleur de lis* red) like those in the President's House at the University of Texas. But the chairs didn't arrive in time for the first Alumni Association function at the house, so I called on our good friend Jim Colvin at UT.

"Could I borrow the red and white chairs from the Meadowbrook house just for one evening?" I asked him. Since no one was living in Meadowbrook house at the time, he quickly agreed to help me out.

142

Chapter 24

Inauguration at Rice

The months surrounding our move from Austin to Houston were hectic indeed. I was busy renovating the President's House, and Norm turned his attention immediately to shoring up the university's finances with the goal of increasing the endowment to make Rice one of the great private universities in the country. Even as Norm was launching endowment building efforts, he was faced with telling the faculty not to expect salary increases for a while.

In addition to our public responsibilities, we were uprooting our two younger daughters from their Austin friends and school activities. This was especially difficult for Sally, who would have begun her senior year at Stephen F. Austin High School. Instead, she was thrown into the new environment of Kincaid as a senior. Her classmates had already formed close friendships and ties — the same kind that Sally had to leave behind in Austin. Many a night I wept silently for my beautiful daughter who was so homesick for Austin. Even now, I regret that we didn't make plans for her to finish high school in Austin. But that's part of the past, the same past that is best left unexamined.

Both Norm and I are grateful to H. Malcolm Lovett for imbuing us with a sense of Rice's history and the vision of what this great university could become. No one alive could do this better than Malcolm Lovett.

His father, Malcolm Odell Lovett, was the first president of Rice (then Rice Institute), and he spent many months in Europe, steeping himself in the lore and the grandeur of Europe's great universities. It was this grand tour that set the course for Rice, both academically and physically. The campus, recognized as one of the most beautiful in the New World, borrows from the Mediterranean. The "college system," where students live and study together in close association with their professors, also follows the European model. In his inaugural talk, Edgar Lovett promised that Rice would one day have "three great divisions: science, humanity, technology." He also promised to "see that the physical aspect of the Institute be one of great beauty."

His son, Malcolm, remembered his father's sojourn in Europe, and made it a point that every president of Rice would make substantially the same trip — to soak up the atmosphere of the European universities and to visit the spiritual roots of Rice.

So we — Norm, Sally, Katy and I — were dispatched on a five-week trip to Europe during our first summer at Rice. It was memorable for all of us in different ways. We went to Germany and France, Scotland and England. While Norm visited the universities and the headquarters of scientific and academic societies, the girls and I visited museums and tried to learn as much as we could about what was going on wherever we were. In Paris we stayed in a penthouse belonging to Herbert Allen, vice-chairman of the Rice Board of Governors and head of Cameron Iron Works. We were just around the corner from the location of the Vietnam Peace Conferences, and we spent hours at the window of the penthouse, watching the comings and goings of delegates to the peace talks. It seemed that at last the war that had torn us all apart had become little more than a matter of grinding out the language of settlement. We were in Paris July 14, Bastille Day, and went to a memorable parade.

We had lunch at the Eiffel Tower, a dinner boat trip on the Rhine with a science group, a motor trip (with a marvelous chauffeur) looking for the Loch Ness monster, caught a glimpse of the queen during a summer visit to Balmoral Castle, and walked all over London. Also, wherever we went, I had to play the part of a forbidding chaperone to my seventeen-year-old, Sally, who had grown beautiful beyond belief, and who caught the ogling eye of young men of every nationality.

We were propelled by air, hydrofoil, across the North Sea to

Inauguration at Rice

Copenhagen, where we spent two or three days. Once, in the Tivoli Gardens, where we stopped to get ice cream cones, five or six young men came up to Norm and said, "Hi, Dr. Hackerman, remember us? We were in your freshman chemistry class."

It was in Copenhagen that I learned to identify the smell of marijuana. Lots of kids were on dope. It saddened me.

We went to Wimbledon, and Katy stood in the middle of a tennis court. In England we rented a car and took long drives around the countryside, getting out to stroll in gardens and out-of-the-way places. Sally left her purse in the car, and it was stolen.

When we returned to Houston, plans were already being made for Norm's inauguration as the fourth president of Rice. Again in the European tradition, inaugurations of presidents at Rice are splendid occasions, with official delegates from universities all over the country, distinguished speakers representing letters, science and arts, and all the ritual of a great occasion. All of our children and grandchildren (only three then) came to Houston for the inauguration and the events surrounding it.

While the inauguration was September 24, 1971, it all began the afternoon before. Promptly at 3:00 P.M., Mr. Lovett appeared at the door of the President's House and presented Norm with the formal summons to appear for his inauguration the following day.

The main speaker at the inaugural ceremonies was Dr. Logan Wilson, former chancellor of the University of Texas System, and at the time president of the American Council on Education in Washington, D.C. As I listened to Dr. Wilson's talk about the place of Rice in the academic firmament and about Norm's qualifications to be president of that university, I had a lump in my throat, so impressed was I with Dr. Wilson's perception of Norm's special qualities.

". . . he has strong leadership qualities that minimize divisiveness and maximize unity of purpose," he said. "Everybody who really cares about the present and future of Rice University should place a high value on leadership of this character."

After Dr. Wilson's speech, Mr. Lovett then placed the ribbon bearing the medallion symbolizing the authority of the presidential office around Norm's neck.

The Time Has Come

I couldn't help but think, as I listened and watched, how touching such a ceremony as this is — so healing and unifying for all the different elements of a university. I remember there was no such ceremony, no ceremony at all, when Norm became president of the University of Texas at Austin.

Was Norm thinking the same thing? He did say in his response, "And so I am brought back to the appropriateness of ceremonies such as this . . . I hope this ceremony will be for you, as it is for me, a symbolic act — a rededication of the aims and purposes of a fine institution as defined by its founder, set in motion so magnificently by its first president, and continued expertly by the second and third presidents . . ."

After the ceremony was over, Jack Maguire, then executive director of the Ex-Students Association at the University of Texas, hugged me and said, "Right man. Right job. Wrong university." Jack had hoped Norm would stay at UT.

Back to the President's House we went, and soon we were embroiled in a domestic crisis. The inaugural dinner, due to begin in just an hour or two, was a black-tie affair. Steve and Mary had come from California, and as Steve began to dress, he discovered that Mary had failed to pack the trousers of his tuxedo. Knowing not to get involved, I said nothing, but, of course, thought to myself, "Why didn't Steve pack his own trousers?"

By that time, all the stores, all the rental shops were closed. Steve had no trousers.

But there's always a solution. I pulled out one of Norm's old tuxedos, ripped them down the back (to make them bigger) and let the hem out (to make them longer). With Addie Mae's expert hand and steam iron, soon Steve was dressed in a tux that included trousers.

To Pat's almost hysterical suggestion that Steve go to the party with no pants, Steve responded, "I can hear Jack Blanton saying now, 'Look, the Hackermans let their idiot son dress himself and come to the party!' "

So, as usual, another Hackerman near-disaster ended in laughter.

Another emergency was yet to come. Giovanna, granddaughter Erin's nurse, flushed Erin's paper diapers down the

146

commode at the President's House. So at 2:00 in the morning, the Roto-Rooter truck was out in front of the house; the roto-rooter was doing its work.

At the gala dinner MacKinlay Kantor spoke for letters, Professor George W. Beadle spoke for science, and Jack Valenti spoke for art. And Norm spoke for me, "I learned a lot . . . from that very attractive girl I met thirty-five years ago who is this equally attractive lady here on my right, who has been a very important counselor and adviser and whose advice I have taken more often than she thinks I have."

And so, as always, everything was worth the trouble.

Chapter 25

Of Cabbages and Kings

Our house — all our houses — were always filled with people: the children's friends, Norm's academic and scientific associates, and my friends who were working with me on various projects. Although one couldn't call this entertaining, and nothing was every very formal, we could put together something good to eat and refreshing to drink very quickly, and the people themselves always furnished the entertainment — good and stimulating conversation.

The circumstances of Norm's increasing responsibilities changed all this. We moved into the University of Texas President's House in 1967, and into the Rice University President's House in 1970. I had to change quickly from a private person with many pop-in friends of all ages to a public person, one who made guest lists and checked them twice, worked up menus and planned their service, and ordered flowers that would create beauty and conversation, even as I tried to quiet a recurring nightmare.

This anxiety dream began soon after we moved into the Meadowbrook house. It was neither long nor complicated, and it would take no Joseph to interpret. I dreamed that the doorbell rang, and a glittery array of guests in formal clothes stood at the front door, having arrived for dinner. As I greeted these elegant people, I remembered that I had failed to go to the grocery store . . .

I embarked on what turned into a career of entertaining: faculty members, administrators, governing board members, alumni, benefactors, politicians, heads of state, ambassadors, royalty, admirals, generals. So ended the era of Gene Hackerman and her tuna fish casseroles and bald lemon pies.

At just about the same time Norm became president of Rice University, Derek C. Bok was named president of Harvard. When Dr. Bok accepted the job, he made it clear to the Harvard Board that his wife (Sissela Bok) had her own career and would not be playing the role of the Harvard president's wife. I had heard this story, and sometimes I thought about it, but not for long. I think Mrs. Bok may have missed a lot of the kind of joy and stimulation I had in getting to know the people who were important to Norm's work. Where else could I have had such an opportunity to watch the interplay of the business and philanthropic worlds with the academic?

What did I do at Rice? Let me give you some statistics.

In the President's House we entertained with lunches, dinners, teas, coffee, student lunches. In all, we fed 3,000 people a year. During the fifteen years we were at Rice, this came to 45,000 people — 90,000 feet walking through the house!

As the official Rice hostess, I found it necessary to:

. . . plan all menus
. . . make up all guest lists
. . . have invitations printed
. . . set up all the tables
. . . launder linens at the house
. . . supervise grounds and garden
. . . run an office and staff

It was good all the way, and even when things didn't quite go by the chart, it gave us much to laugh about. And a chart there was. After the invitations were out and the menu was planned, we prepared the house for the best movement of the guests, so mixing would be easy. The guest lists were diverse, so people of many different interests and accomplishments would have a chance to exchange views and understand each other better.

I have a basic concept about entertaining — particularly in one's home. The guest list should be made up, if possible, of people who are congenial with each other, or have the potential to be. Sometimes, however, when you are dealing with people you don't know well, as a president's wife often does, mistakes can be made. I made two such mistakes, both memorable, the first at the University of Texas, and the next at Rice.

Even when he was president, Norm always taught chemistry and we stayed in touch with his chemistry colleagues. One evening in Austin we invited the chemistry professors and their wives to our house for dinner and bridge.

Since I rarely gossip, no one ever tells me anything, so I was unaware of the undercurrents in my house that evening. The dinner went fine. Then we sat down to play bridge. It was party bridge, so as the game progressed, the partners changed from table to table. The hostess has no control over who plays at which table after the beginning. I was concentrating on my own game when the uproar began.

All of a sudden the wife of one of the chemists very loudly said to the wife of another, "Take your goddamn hands off my husband!" Then she jumped up and ran outside. I followed her. Sobbing, she told me, "I'm going home." And she did.

Meanwhile, her husband had come outside, where he promptly threw up on the lawn.

I went back into the room where the other guests were no longer playing bridge. They were standing up, reaching for their coats, and mumbling things like, "Dinner was wonderful." Then they hurried away.

So Norm and I picked up the dishes, put them in the dishwasher, and climbed into our bed with great relief that it was over.

Tomorrow was another day, however. When Norm got home he asked, "Why did you invite the Blanks and the Blanks to the same party?"

He said he had had a number of chemistry faculty ask him, "Why did Gene invite them? Everybody knows what's going on."

But Gene didn't know. Nobody had told me anything, and I don't believe Norm knew either, though he said, "Well, everybody in chemistry knows that Blank is fooling around with Blank's wife."

And so it goes.

Of Cabbages and Kings

The incident at Rice happened at a football game. As the wife of the president, I had been given the job of filling sixteen seats in our box in the stadium at every home game, every other week. Two of these sixteen seats were ours. That left seven couples to invite. Being new to Houston, I did not know a great many Houstonians.

Before each football game, we invited two hundred people for a buffet in the President's House. Included in this pre-game luncheon or dinner were the fourteen people who would share our box.

On this particular occasion, I invited Senator and Mrs. Lloyd Bentsen and Mr. and Mrs. George Bush. On my list, George Bush was identified as a "prominent businessman who resided in Houston." I had seated the Bushes and the Bentsens directly in front of Norm and me.

Either I didn't know or had forgotten that Mr. Bush had challenged Mr. Bentsen for the Senate seat in 1964 — and lost.

The game proceeded, and the two couples in front of us seemed to be friendly with each other and having a good time.

The next day our phone rang several times with gracious people gently telling me they thought I ought to know that Senator Bentsen had competed with and defeated Mr. Bush in the race for the United States Senate!

*   *   *

Both the University of Texas at Austin and Rice University had many eminent faculty members, persons who had published or who had executed works of art or brought other honor to themselves and their university. I borrowed faculty books and faculty art to be displayed in the President's House. Before a party, I placed books by faculty authors who were invited to this particular party in strategic places on tables inside the traffic flow. It was a great conversation piece for someone to comment on a book a colleague had written.

Flower arrangements also serve as conversation pieces. With the cooperation of talented florists, the arrangements on serving tables and throughout the house always included some unusual

151

blossom or greenery, something that might pose a question to be answered.

Most of the work for a party was begun the week before, and the intense activity continued up until noon of the day of a dinner.

In planning the menus I was very conscious of people's varying tastes, and was aware of the more common food allergies; for example, some people have violent reactions to shellfish. I usually had two entrées — one at each end of the dining table. One would be a crab casserole or fish or shrimp, and the other would be beef stroganoff or another dish using chicken or beef.

As a precaution, I tried to stand near the dining table and indicate to the guests what each of the entrées contained. Also, I always invited a medical doctor to our dinners. Houston, with its world-class medical center, has hordes of doctors, and many of them are Rice alumni.

There's many a slip between cup and lip, however. On one occasion, a guest took his helping from the shrimp casserole. He must have tasted the shrimp as he walked away from the table because when he got to me, he was choking.

"Are you ill?" I asked. When he nodded, we quickly showed him the way to the bathroom, and in a few minutes he was all right.

Another precaution against party misfortune was to keep the hall closet empty so women could stow their purses in it and conveniently pick them up as they were leaving. Purses with shoulder straps are particularly hazardous under chairs, just sitting there trying to catch a foot.

*   *   *

Shortly after we arrived at Rice, the Shepherd School of Music acquired a new dean. The trustees, with our participation, hosted a reception for Dean and Mrs. Sam Jones at the River Oaks Country Club. The invitation list included much of Houston's glittering social and cultural establishment. This occasion was primarily a Houston community affair, and the new dean had yet to be introduced socially to the Rice faculty.

Immediately after Dean Jones performed his first concert, Norm and I hosted a reception in the President's House for 500 people, the number of seats in the concert hall. Five hundred guests comprise a large crowd for a reception where everyone arrives at once.

I arranged for the guests to enter the front door of the house. Coffee and sweets were served from the dining room table. The bartender was at his post at the bar in the serving area. No tables were set up in the house, and the guests were gently persuaded to move to the garden to enjoy their refreshments. For the only time while we were at Rice, we left our garden gate unlocked and open, so departing guests could take the brick pathway around the house to their cars.

By that time I had solved the mosquito problem, which plagues Houston in the spring and summer. We had the area sprayed just before a party in the garden, and I set up citronella candles in colorful glass globes strategically throughout the area.

*   *   *

Rice maintains the "college system." Every entering freshman is assigned to one of the eight colleges on campus, even if he or she does not live on campus. Each college has a master, who with wife or husband (women faculty members are sometimes masters) lives on campus and takes meals with the students in the college. Thus every student has daily informal access to a professor.

Because we, too, lived on campus, I enjoyed the contact with the wives of the masters. From time to time we had small parties at the President's House just for the masters and their families. One time when I spent a few days at Lakeway, I stopped by the greatest barbeque place in the Hill Country, Cowtown, and picked up barbeque ribs, sausage and brisket for a spring masters party. Marion Hicks, who was in charge of food service at Rice, heated the barbeque for us and added potato salad and cole slaw to make the meal a true barbeque. The children of the masters came, wearing their bathing suits. We all had a good time.

Also, from time to time I would drop in for luncheon at the colleges — both the men's and the women's. I enjoyed randomly picking out a table, and asking, "May I sit here?" and entering conversation with my table mates. One thing that always amazed me was how smart the students were, and how they took their intelligence for granted. After I had been at Rice about a year, I was eating lunch at one of the men's colleges, and the conversation went something like this:

"I'm Mrs. Hackerman."

"Yes, we know who you are."

Then I said, "I've been here through one football season, and I couldn't help but notice that many students don't attend the games. I'm surprised that you aren't more excited about Rice and about its truly outstanding student body."

"Mrs. Hackerman," the young man answered, "we all know we're smart. We don't have to talk about it all the time."

From that conversation I understood that, unlike the *nouveau riche* or the first person in their families to go to college, the students at Rice, as a whole, took higher education and intellectual development as a matter of course, and not as something to be talked about all the time.

While most of our Rice parties were held at the President's House, this was not always the rule. For example, Rice has about 300 freshmen each year. We held the New Students' reception at the Art Department one fall, and it worked very well, providing an opportunity for the incoming students to wander around among the easels and see the work of faculty and other students on the walls.

Virtually every social event at the President's House and on the campus were Rice's parties, and not mine, and I tried to make them showcases for the university. For example, the Shepherd Society is a group organized to attract support for the music program at Rice. On one occasion, Mr. Lovett gave me an invitation list for a party at the President's House for the Shepherd Society. Somehow we missed sending an invitation to an important person on the list. When Mr. Lovett called to tell me of the omission, I hand-delivered the invitation to the woman. I wanted everything to work well, and it usually did.

An example of the sometimes complicated preparations are the notes on our luncheon in honor of the Duke of Edinburgh.

Soon after the International Scientific Symposium on Tropical Forests and Primates accepted Rice's invitation to hold its 1981 meeting in Houston, one of the Rice trustees suggested to

Norm that it would be nice if we "had a little luncheon" for Prince Philip, president of the World Wildlife Fund International.

"*Well* . . . all right," I agreed. So we began the adventure of getting ready for royalty.

The British consul general wasted no time in letting me know what was proper and what was not. There were admonitions like this: "His Royal Highness DOES NOT SMOKE." Guests at a party he attends should not smoke. The consul general brought me written materials covering security, etiquette and protocol. For the next four weeks, these were my bible.

We learned that Prince Philip's official title is "His Royal Highness, The (note the capital T) Prince Philip, Duke of Edinburgh." We noted in the "Protocol tips," to "H.R.H. The Duke of Edinburgh." In press releases, after the first reference, he may be referred to as "The Duke of Edinburgh," "His Royal Highness," or "Prince Philip."

Also, we learned that official royal protocol dictates that one should not speak to a member of the Royal family until presented to him, or addressed by him. "Prince Philip is usually fairly informal at World Wildlife events," said the consul general, "but it is nonetheless a good idea for someone he knows to present any new people to him like this, 'Your Royal Highness, may I present So-and-So?' The person being presented should then shake hands and bow. Ladies may bow or curtsy if they prefer." At our luncheon Dr. Hackerman made the presentations.

Ladies who are not British subjects are not expected to curtsy on being presented to H.R.H., but if they wish to, it will be recognized as a pleasant courtesy.

The protocol instructions had this to say about dress: "His Royal Highness normally wears an ordinary suit, but is happy to wear casual clothes for field trips, or black tie or dinner jacket for more formal occasions. He prefers not to have to wear white tie or evening coat with tails, although he will if the occasion requires it."

Dietary restrictions. I needed to know this in preparing the menu. Off limits for Prince Philip is shellfish (prawns, shrimp, crab, etc.). "H.R.H. is quite adventurous and would eat most food of the country he is visiting," said the official instructions. "But no berries, please. No shellfish.

"The prince's favorite drink is a dry martini (gin and vermouth), but he also drinks tomato juice, wine and on informal occasions, beer." We were told he does not drink much and almost nothing until the evening. We served wine before lunch, but I don't remember if he drank any.

With the above in mind, I came up with a menu of some of my favorite dishes: salad of artichoke and palm hearts with vinaigrette, poached salmon with dill sauce, fresh asparagus with pimiento, parsleyed new potatoes, hot rolls, lemon soufflé.

We used our regular student waiters for Prince Philip's luncheon. We liked to have student waiters so our visitors could have contact with our students. We were proud of them. On this occasion, of course, we had more students wanting to be waiters than we needed. Each of them had to be cleared by Scotland Yard Security as well as national, state, and city security. After Norm presented the guests to the prince at the reception in the living room before lunch was served, I asked H.R.H. if he would care to meet the student waiters. He did, and this was a high point for them.

During our fifteen years at Rice, most of the food at our parties in the President's House was served buffet style, with sometimes as many as 200 guests for meals and 500 for receptions. We had only sixty-four guests for Prince Philip's luncheon, a seated meal. The consul general asked that we seat all the guests before the prince entered the dining room. Also, no one was to leave while Prince Philip was still there.

With menu settled and guest list drawn, I spent many hours trying to decide on the seating of sixty-four guests — eight tables, with eight at each table. My protractor worked overtime, drawing and redrawing. Each circle on the paper represented a table, and on each circle I wrote eight names. The guest list included Houston notables as well as world-renowned scholars who were speakers at the international seminar.

The first name I placed on each circle/table was that of one of the speakers. After that, I tried to place members of the Rice faculty and people from the Rice community who had interests similar to the speaker's.

Of Cabbages and Kings

I worried some that everyone couldn't sit at the table with Prince Philip, and mentioned this concern to Mrs. Malcolm Lovett. "Oh, that's all right," said Martha Lovett. "I'd rather sit with Walter Cronkite." And so she did. Walter was one of the seminar speakers. His wife, Betsy, was with him, as were their daughter Kathy and her husband, William Ikard. My dear birdwatcher friend, Dorie Ellsworth, sat at the table with Dr. Roger Tory Peterson, author of Dorie's constant companion, *A Field Guide to the Birds*. They had a fine conversation about avian conservation.

I arranged the tables so that everyone could see the prince. To make this possible, we had to get the regular furniture out of the house. So we rented a U-Haul trailer, loaded it with the furniture, and parked it out of sight behind the garage. This gave me three large connecting rooms with a view of the garden and space for eight tables and their attending chairs. Each student waiter was assigned to one table only.

All in all, our party was a memorable success. Prince Philip was charming, and everything went smoothly. But Norm and I couldn't go to the formal dinner for the prince at the Warwick Hotel that night. We had to move the furniture back into the house and get ready for a pre-football game buffet for 200 people the next day!

As my newspaper friend Linda Barr put it, "The prince should have known that in Texas, football is king."

Chapter 26

Academia is for the Birds

usk had just fallen. The campus and our house were peaceful. The birds were cozily entrenched in the fifty live oaks around the President's House. Katy and Max Bunch, in tennis whites, had come home from playing tennis. A gentleman always, Max jumped out of the door of his car, slammed it shut, and went around to help Katy out her door. The second he slammed the door, the birds woke up and let loose, spraying poor Max. There he stood, wiping the cowbirds' guano off hair, shirt, and arms.

Katy, never one to suffer in silence, flung herself through the front door, halfway up the staircase, and without greeting or ceremony said, "Tell Daddy I'm leaving. I can't stand those birds any longer!"

"Wait," said I. "I'm going with you. Just let me clean up Max."

I pushed him into Norm's study, where "Himself" was sitting at his desk, and said, "Help Max clean up in your bathroom."

Katy didn't leave, and neither did I, but we had simultaneously come to the same conclusion. We couldn't stand the cowbirds any longer. She was tired of her friends teasing her about the hazards of walking up our drive, and I was tired of fighting them.

Usually my philosophy about flying creatures is live and let live. If they leave me alone, I'll leave them alone. But these birds did not leave me alone. They filled every branch on every tree surrounding the President's House. One evening I turned out

Academia is for the Birds

the lights in our bedroom and peered out the window into the large live oak directly in front of it. I counted ten branches in my line of vision where roosted approximately fifty birds on each branch, snuggling together to keep warm. One hundred beady eyes stared at me from each branch. The scene reminded me of the movie *The Birds,* and I felt physically ill.

The cowbirds arrived at Rice December 15 and flew away March 15. Now I understand what those poor people at Capistrano have to go through every year.

The stench was incredible. In the mornings it was impossible to walk anywhere under the trees where the cowbirds slept. Their guano covered the walks, the grass, the driveways. Every morning, promptly at eight, the first of the gardeners arrived and began washing off shrubs, grass, and walkways, handholding the hose. It was a mess.

In mid-December, a Houston television station reported on the evening news that an estimated one million cowbirds had settled on the Rice campus.

On their way to the library or evening classes, the women from Jones and Brown colleges had to cross the quadrangle diagonally, and they found it necessary to carry umbrellas to protect themselves and their clothing from bird excrement.

Once the birds were in the trees and settled down, any noise disturbed them. And any time they were disturbed, diarrhea ensued. Even the scuffling of feet on the sidewalk caused a response demanding umbrella protection.

In the mornings, a million or more wings flapped with a clapping sound as they took off for the rice fields near Katy, having already awakened our household by starting to chirp in the pre-dawn light.

When we went out to get the *Houston Post* from the front porch, we found it pristine, but the grass and walks were another story.

I decided early on that if I were going to control the birds instead of the birds controlling me, I had to learn everything I could about them. So I began my research. I watched them. I learned that if I made enough noise, they wouldn't land in my trees. I also learned that they stopped flying wherever they were

159

The Time Has Come

when it got dark, so if they weren't in the trees by the time it was completely dark, we were safe for that night.

Thus began the implementation of my first solution — banging two saucepans together. I banged saucepans together in the back garden, and Addie Mae did the same in the front. But the birds held strategy sessions during the day.

"How can we ruin Mrs. Hackerman's dinner party tonight?" the Chief of the Birds would ask. "Well, the guests are expected to arrive at seven," a young bird on his way up in the academic birdland would answer. "Let's have a full-court assault, an all-bird dump on the ladies in their finery."

And so they did. We have hustled many an arriving guest to the bathroom for a round of ice water sponging to remove the tell-tale bombs the birds dropped.

It wouldn't do.

So my lieutenant in this war, Addie Mae, and I went on the offensive. We went to Foley's and bought ammunition — a dozen rounds of stew pans. Thirty minutes before the guests were due, we went into the yard and started banging the pans together with all our might. The frightened birds rose from their perches in mighty clouds and flew away. The stew pans worked, and Addie Mae and I used them steadily for months, and sporadically thereafter.

While our stew pans were the most reliable audio weapons against the Invasion of the Birds, we in fact launched a multi-fronted war. We had the best minds at Rice University working on the problem.

I passed along the results of my research to some of the engineers at Rice, thinking they could certainly come up with something that would scare the birds.

Norm put his assistant, Russ Pittman, to work on the problem. One evening Russ sent over a flat-bed truck complete with a mounted fan pointing skyward. This fan was about forty inches in diameter, about the size of the propelling fan on a swamp buggy. The fan was designed to blow the birds off their perches. Well, it did, for a moment. The birds would lift off, leaving always a deposit, then settle back on the branches. The fan only succeeded in making the birds more nervous, and thus managed to produce even worse cases of diarrhea.

The Music Department provided recordings — cassettes — of deafening noises which we played in the evenings to scare the birds away. While playing the noise tape freed Addie Mae and me, it also had its downside. One evening, as we were playing the cassette at full-blast, the telephone rang. A co-ed voice said, "Mrs. Hackerman, I just can't study with all that racket going on."

I invited her to come over for a handful of ear plugs. (That's another story: We had a carton of 120 dozen ear plugs, courtesy of the U.S. government. When Norm went to Antarctica, his hosts, the National Science Foundation, issued him ear plugs to protect him from the roar of the Navy plane. They issued him not just a pair of ear plugs, but enough for a lifetime of noise.)

Another problem with the noise tapes was that we had to engage a babysitter/cassette-changer when we went out at night — to turn off the cassette player after the birds had flown away and, presumably, found another place to roost.

The story of our noise-making tapes got around Houston. The rector of Christ Church Cathedral asked for a set of cassettes to drive the birds away from the Cathedral's premises. One day I got a plaintive call from the Cathedral: "Your tape doesn't work . . . ." I referred the caller to the Music Department.

As it turned out, our homemade and Music Department remedies were more effective, humane, and economical than the solutions offered by the Engineer Department, one of the best in the nation.

The next plan was to drop net parachutes from helicopters on top of the trees in the quadrangle, thus forming a shield against the birds. But parachutes are made of solid nylon, not net, so this plan, too, was doomed to failure. So the helicopters dropped long scarves of netting over the trees, reminding me of the long streams of toilet paper high school students used to string high in the trees at the homes of football heroes and the most popular girls. But the netting dropped in the trees became bird traps, and we often found carcasses of birds that had been strangled by getting caught up in them.

The stench from these dead birds lingered long after the

161

surviving birds had flown away for the summer. The university maintenance people came with a cherry picker to pluck the carcasses from the trees, but still the noxious aroma remained. The cherry picker didn't find all the dead birds.

During the Invasion of the Birds, our parties took on a tone of their own. We met our guests with raincoats and umbrellas so they could walk to our front door without being pelted by bird excrement.

Then there was the streaker who made his dashing run across the campus. When the campus police picked him up, they found a bird had pelted his bareness with a glob that wasn't chewing gum.

Finally, the birds packed up their nests and moved on, but only to settle just a few blocks away from Rice, at Shady Side.

Chapter 27

Women and Cars

onfrontation is not my style. I never burned a bra or marched in a parade to promote the Equal Rights Amendment. But my heart has been with women who have no options, those women in poverty working against great odds to keep their children in school and food on the table.

I was personally annoyed and affronted by the fact that, in much of the United States, women could not make contracts on their own, or own property, or make any significant purchase or legal decision without the signature of their husbands. So I was particularly elated when the state of Texas removed these disabilities on November 7, 1972, the day when women's signatures became as legally viable as the signatures of the men to whom they were married. The wording of the new law read, "Equality under the law shall not be denied or abridged because of sex, race, color, creed, or national origin."

I had always thought it ironic that Texans (male Texans, to be sure) took such pride in the reliable character of their spoken word, their very handshake, when even a woman's signature was not considered valid.

In 1973, when I went to buy a station wagon in Houston, it never occurred to me that someone would try to stop me. (My uncle had died and left me a legacy of $150,000, which I had put into a savings and loan account.)

I went to a Chevrolet agency to look for a station wagon.

163

The Time Has Come

Even before I arrived, I had a good idea of the kind of car I wanted, and I soon found it.

"Yes, I'll take that one," I said to the young salesman. I believe the total price was $8,000, and I had no car to trade. "I'd like to write you a check for $2,000, and carry the balance for a year," I said. This seemed agreeable to the salesman, who left the showroom to take my proposal to the office upstairs.

In a few minutes he returned with a paper in hand, saying, "Take this home and get your husband to sign it."

"No," I said. "*My* signature is legal in the state of Texas." The young man left again, and came back with another request, "They want your Social Security number and bank account number." I gave those to him.

When he returned, he again insisted that I get my husband's signature.

Angry by this time, I said, "Either your manager lets me sign these papers or I'll sue him."

Again the young man scurried away. When he returned he was accompanied by a rotund manager-type with a cigar clamped between his teeth.

"Now, little lady," said he, "your husband needs to okay this contract."

"I'll sue you," I said.

"Now, now, little lady . . ."

"You didn't ask for my husband's signature on the check," I said quietly, becoming more angry every minute.

Noting that I was not to be bluffed, the manager assured me that they would get the paperwork out while the salesman and I decided on a delivery plan. Getting Norm's signature was mentioned no more.

The salesman did bring the station wagon and the papers for *me* to sign. He ate supper with us. He told my secretary, Bernice Stevenson, "I never met a woman like that before in my life."

Chapter 28

Five Friends

Perhaps it is so that love can be "at first sight," but the same is not true of friendship. Of all relationships, that between friends is the slowest growing, and must be nurtured and tended, like a green young plant. Friendship has to age slowly, like fine wine. Good friendships are built in small increments of shared laughter, common enemies, exchanged favors, and adventurous expeditions to fight windmills or discover perfect fossils. Friends share their quiet with you when you are in pain and their pleasure when you are filled with joy.

God hit the right chord when He said, "Be still and know that I am God." This can be paraphrased, "Be still and know that I am your Friend."

We moved to Houston and Rice University in 1970, and I hated leaving Austin. I was one of a coterie of friends who had grown up together since 1945 — a quarter-century of helping each other's children grow up, of shared laughter and heartache. Oh, how I hated to leave my friends.

Looking back to the Houston years now, I see that I knew many people I enjoyed being with, many who enriched my life, but I count four women — each younger than I — as my particular friends, ones I carry in my heart always. They are Carolyn Wallace, Mona Stebbings, Grace Bunch, and Dorie Ellsworth. Two were connected with Rice, and two I met through other activities.

I've thought a lot about what made these particular four

women so important to me, besides, of course, that they are nice people and fun to be with. The common quality they share is that they all are experts in fields I enjoyed and wanted to know more about. They all have consuming interests and considerable enthusiasm for learning and doing. They all enjoy the outdoors and nature — hills and beaches and gardens.

Grace Bunch knows everything about books. She often goes to publishers' markets, reads voraciously, is conversant about authors and how they find their material and develop it.

Mona Stebbings can sew gorgeous garments and knows everything about fabric. She once worked for the dressmaker who sewed by appointment to the Queen of England. She is a magnificent cook, and she taught me to make the divine English trifle. No ingredient is too elusive for Mona to track down, no trouble is too much for her delicate kitchen magic.

Carolyn Wallace knows everything about fossils and shells, and content not only to find them, she studies them under a microscope and shares what she sees with us.

Dorie Ellsworth's specialized knowledge concerns medicine, nutrition and health, and birds.

My own passions are for architecture and building, flowers and gardens, children and children's causes, books and the worlds they open. They are eclectic interests, one might say.

The five of us, however, are interested in all of these subjects and activities, so when we are together a great deal of conversational excitement prevails.

Mona, the wife of Dr. Ronald Stebbings, a physics professor at Rice, served as liaison between the Rice community and the Houston Symphony Orchestra. We had Symphony Society functions at the President's House, and it was through these functions that Mona and I began our friendship.

How can I describe her — this transplanted Brit? Full-figured. Very pretty. A blonde and blue-eyed English lady. Sparkle. Sense of humor. Even when she was angry for some righteous reason, never have I seen Mona vitriolic.

Although she was born in England and I on Maryland's eastern shore, we laughed sometimes that we must have been sisters in some past life. One day as a rainstorm ended, I remarked, quoting my grandmother, "Look, the rain is over. It's getting lighter in the West."

"*What* did you say?" Mona interrupted. "That is exactly what my mother said as rain began to taper off."

Mona is also the kind of friend who is ready for spontaneous adventure. I might remark, "It would be nice to go to Galveston early tomorrow morning and walk on the beaches."

"Let's do it," she would answer. She would show up the next morning with a Thermos of coffee and some finger snacks — cheese, crackers, etc. After walking and picking up sacks of shells, we'd sit on a dune and eat our snacks. Sometimes we talked and talked and talked, stumbling over each's words, trying to tell our thoughts and ideas. Other times, we spoke hardly at all. That is another of my definitions of friendship — friends don't have to talk. They can enjoy silence together or can pick up unfinished conversations left hanging when they separated years ago.

Then we would go to Guido's for a seafood lunch, then back to Houston and our work.

While Mona is like a rock, steady and strong, Carolyn Wallace is like a sparkler, effervescent and daring, bright. Carolyn is always attempting the undo-able. She takes a chance on anything. Often she surprises us, and accomplishes the impossible.

Carolyn was the director of the Rice Alumni Association. Soon after we arrived at Rice and got settled in the President's House, I called Carolyn, invited her over for a cup of coffee, and asked her if there was something I could help her with. Since Carolyn not only attempts the undo-able herself, but also encourages others to do the same, she of course had something for me to try.

"Let's activate the Dallas alums," she suggested. "We need a hard-working, large alumni club in Dallas." Carolyn's husband, Bruce, is an architect and was in touch with a group of architect friends in Dallas, and Carolyn knew the hard-core Rice boosters there.

"Go with me to Dallas," suggested Carolyn. "We'll get a small group together at the Brook Hollow Country Club to meet you."

I demurred, suggesting that the alums would want to hear Norm talk, not meet me. But Carolyn had a plan; she was saving Norm for later — for the big crowd. She wanted me to go now and meet her friends. She convinced me, mostly because I felt I could learn so much from these ex-students about how Rice was while they were there, about their memories of their *alma mater.*

So that's what we did. Carolyn and I went to Dallas and met with six or eight couples at the club. Carolyn proposed a membership drive in Dallas with these couples taking the lead. It worked, and soon the large group was in place. And sure enough, Norm went to speak with them about Rice's future and what they could do to keep the university great.

I was able to help in another small way. I had an entertainment allowance at Rice for university activities. This allowance was used for functions at the President's House for faculty, students, alumni, and friends of Rice. Since the Dallas alumni could not conveniently travel to Houston for an organization meeting, I told Carolyn we could pick up some of the costs in Dallas for the get-together.

Carolyn, adventurous and friendly, retains a youthful trust in virtually all persons and even in the forces of nature. Once she, her children, and her sister-in-law were at Rockport when hurricane warnings began swirling over the airwaves. Cautious as I am, I would have been out of there in a hurry and on the highway to Houston, but not Carolyn. She decided they didn't really have to leave.

When the winds began to howl and the voices on the radio reached higher pitches, she decided they had better get back to the mainland.

As she backed out of the garage, she bumped into some kind of obstruction. The damage seemed negligible, but she drove to a service station in any case, since the gas gauge was on empty. She pulled into a long line of cars. She then noticed a low tire, so in addition to the gasoline, she asked that her tire be changed. But the trunk door wouldn't open as a result of the small collision.

Carolyn had a decision to make — they had to stay in Rockport at the service station, or risk driving back to Houston on a low tire. She decided to ride out the storm, so the two women and four children huddled under tables at the service station/cafe until the storm passed over.

Five Friends

Carolyn tells the story often, and it illustrates part of her aura of a charmed life.

During recent years Carolyn has had a painful back operation, cared for her mother until she died, worked out her grief then by caring for an elderly aunt, and, of course, heaped her continuing devotion on her own family.

As I write about each of these dear friends, tears rise to my eyes, thinking of their courage and joyousness and the happy times we have had together.

While Mona and Carolyn were Rice campus friends, I met Grace through Katy.

Katy and Max, Grace's son, were in the sixth grade together at Kincaid. Quite often Katy invited Max to play tennis with her on the Rice courts. Neither was old enough to drive, so one afternoon Grace and Max brought Katy home from school, and the children played tennis. Grace was waiting in her car for the tennis set to end when I went out and invited her into the house. We had a cup of tea, as I recall, and thus began a friendship of our own, separate and distinct from our children's friendship, which itself continues even as they have each married others and have their own families in separate cities.

Grace and I have played the game, "What would you have done, what career would you have followed if you could have done anything you wanted to?"

Grace's answer is always, "I would have liked to be a lawyer." And what a good lawyer she would have made. Research-oriented and a problem solver, she was the manager of the office of a partnership of orthopedic physicians in Houston.

She was the one who took immediate action when my foot, which had been troubling me, became swollen, and I developed a high fever from the infection. She got me in to see an orthopedic specialist in Twelve Oaks Tower and I was admitted into Twelve Oaks Hospital, where I at last got some relief.

Grace's position with the medical partnership came through Dr. McReynolds, a principal, for whom she started working just after she graduated from Rice. In fact, she became so important to the office that when Max was born and Grace wanted to stay at

169

home with him, Dr. McReynolds moved office furniture and files to the Bunch home so Grace could continue to work.

The person I go to if I want information — information about any and everything — is Grace. All I have to say is, "I wonder what the derivative is . . ." or "I wonder what happened to So-and-So . . ." If Grace doesn't have the information in her head or at her fingertips, she makes a thorough research project out of it. The next time I see her, she will give me the information I had wondered about.

During our last months at Rice, several family tragedies befell Grace. A favorite aunt, a sister, and Bowden, the name Grace used for a woman who had been her mentor through the years, all died within an extraordinarily short time. These deaths touched her deeply, not only because of the emotional losses of the important female figures in her life, but because she was named executrix of the estates and had enormous financial responsibilities to their survivors. She rented an office over a store on River Oaks Drive in order to handle all the estate work she had to do.

Shortly after we moved back to Austin, Grace's mother also died, and another of Grace's close friends, the manager of the Galleria in Houston, developed cancer. I remember how touched I was when Grace visited me in Austin. She threw her arms around me, and said, "Now don't *you* up and die on me." By that time Grace had become superstitious that any woman she loved would die.

Dorie Ellsworth entered my life through an introduction from Mona Stebbings. Mona invited me to a small luncheon for some of her Houston friends. My circle in Houston up until then was almost exclusively Rice-related.

Dorie looked smashing that day — very elegant, lovely makeup. My recollections of that first meeting include such fragments as . . . hair in a chignon . . . infectious sense of humor . . . lots of sparkling white teeth . . . a pocketful of great stories . . .

Dorie's husband had an investment business. A trained surgical nurse, she had met him while he was her patient. They married after he left the hospital and had one son who also attended Kincaid with Katy and Max, although he was a few years younger than they.

Dorie and Grace, along with Carolyn and Mona, became fre-

170

quent visitors to our retreat at Lakeway — sometimes there were just the five of us, and other times with four or five other guests. These rather large house parties were possible because I had finished building the second house at Lakeway and still owned the first, next door. We could easily accommodate four to six people in each house. A gate in a low wrought-iron fence between the houses could bring us all together within one and a half minutes.

Dorie's wonderful sense of humor kept us all laughing on many occasions. On one of these expeditions the group included several Rice professors' wives — one from engineering, one from chemistry, along with the athletic director's wife and the wife of the ROTC director.

We were all sitting around in one of the bedrooms — some on the floor, others on the bed, still others in chairs, reminiscent of an after lights-out dorm party. We were discussing makeup, and of course Dorie became the center of this talk because she always looked so elegant and beautifully turned-out.

"Anybody can look gorgeous," said Dorie, and began the most amazing facial striptease. She wiped off her lipstick, pulled off her false eyelashes, and, by golly, took off her chignon and slung it across the bed.

"All is illusion," said Dorie. "All is illusion." After that, we all spruced ourselves up. Beautiful Dorie shared her secrets.

It had been several years since I had seen Dorie when Addie Mae, my daughters and I went to Max's wedding in Houston. As the Hackerman women were escorted to our seats, I saw a very beautiful head of hair up ahead. The hair was now gray, but even from the back I knew at once it belonged to Dorie Ellsworth. No one else could emulate that style and chic.

Another Lakeway visit I particularly remember was in a January. January was a slow month for me at Rice — just after the Christmas holidays, when students were returning, but we hadn't begun a lot of entertaining. It seemed a good time to go to Lakeway with Mona, Carolyn, Grace, and Dorie. So we took the better part of a week to play and recharge our batteries.

This particular time was our third trip together to Lakeway. The weather was cold, but we donned jackets and slacks and took walks, stopping to hunt fossils and pick red leaves from sumac trees.

The weather turned sunny, so we set up a croquet game in the yard. What fun we had! We drank wine, then tried to hit the ball through the wickets. We laughed and made jokes. It was one of those idyllic times of good companionship that none of us will forget.

Another memorable trip was our Halley's Comet adventure. My telescope was stored at Lakeway, but had not been set up. A young woman professor of astronomy at Rice came up from Houston and set it up for us, and the five of us watched the comet from our hilltop.

Our explorations have included the sky, the earth, and many of the earth's living things — the birds and flowers, their beauty deepened by our own *joie de vivre*.

Chapter 29

Rockport

N orm always left house hunting and buying to me. This may be a subtle compliment, suggesting that he trusts me in such weighty matters, but I believe it is more likely because he is not interested, and never has been, in anything about houses. He has said on a number of occasions that for him, all a house needed was a good bathroom, a comfortable bed, and a kitchen where he could have cake and milk before he went to sleep!

But when I bought the house in Rockport, my friend Carolyn Wallace thought I might have gone too far.

Carolyn Wallace and her husband Bruce had the use of a condominium in the Rockport Yacht and Tennis Club Complex. The condo was owned by Bruce's architectural partnership, with each partner allowed certain times to use it.

One day, Carolyn invited me to go with her to Rockport. She had a meeting to attend nearby, and said we would be gone two days. I agreed to go, and while she went to her meetings I walked around the area, enjoying the open water of the bay. I found it restful and peaceful and very beautiful.

I have always been interested in houses of all kinds — row houses, condos, beach houses, duplexes, converted garages, large houses, small houses, Colonial houses, Cape Cod saltboxes on the shores of Massachusetts, and plantation mansions on the deltas. All are different and all are of interest to me.

I had done a lot of research on the new phenomenon, the large condominium complex, with individual ownership of pri-

173

vate homes and shared ownership of the property on which the homes are built.

I discovered such a complex in Rockport, one in which I was interested, so I located the developer, who was also an owner, and asked if any of the houses were for sale. He pointed out one he thought might be available, and I called the owner from his office. The house was in fact for sale. It was completely furnished, and listed in the rental pool, so that I could rent it out whenever I wanted. The owner was asking $50,000, a good price in the 1970s, and I decided to buy it.

But Carolyn was worried to death when she heard what I had done.

"Dr. Hackerman will be angry with you," she said, "and he'll fire me."

"Don't worry about it," I told her. She couldn't understand my calm, but I knew Norm.

Still Carolyn wasn't convinced. When we returned to Houston, she insisted on going into the house with me — to protect me, I suppose. Anyway, Norm came out of his office to greet us, and I told him, "I bought a house at Rockport."

"Oh," he said. And that was that.

I kept the house for a year, and rented it out for four months, the income from which made the payments on the property for the whole year. When I was offered $65,000 for the place, I sold it. (I held it a year and a day so it would qualify for capital gains.)

During that year, I had great fun taking Steve and his family to fish on the pier. I also took my close Rice friends, Mona, Grace, Dorie, and others, for stays there. We always had a pleasant time, and many small adventures. Dorie liked to fish and was successful at it. I recall us cooking some of her catch, and discovering we had no lemon. Instead, we squeezed grapefruit juice on the fish. It tasted wonderful, and we felt we had made a culinary discovery.

The children also used the Rockport place several times, with Steve and Mary going down for weekends to fish.

The scenery continued to enchant me. The trees were arthritic, with many strange twists and bends, reminiscent of William Blake's paintings at the Tate in London. And the sandy strip

174

Rockport

behind the house was a shell collector's paradise. I still have remnants of these collections at our house at Lakeway.

Norm even came with us once, and stayed overnight. It was Christmas, and we had Wendy and Erin along. But nothing was open, and there was nowhere to eat! Starved, we drove home the next morning.

As all my children know, their father rarely came to any house we had other than the one we lived in. He is not an outdoor man, and neither is he play-oriented. He doesn't play golf, or tennis, or like to boat, as all the children did at Lakeway while they were growing up. But he always came to see us when we were away, and ate a meal, and perhaps spent a night, then went back to town.

The townhouse in Austin was his roost! He used it as a hotel on his many short trips to Austin. I kept a set of P.J.'s, a robe, and slippers there for both of us, so we never had to carry luggage, and this made trips to Austin especially nice, with the townhouse very convenient to U.T., the airport, the Capitol, and downtown.

I enjoyed our experiences with the house at Rockport, and the townhouse, just as I have found pleasure in all our homes. But of all our houses since 1968 — the President's House at UT, the President's House at Rice University, our two houses at Lakeway, the Malibu House, Rockport, and townhouse on Pecos Square — of all except our current home, 2001 Pecos, *it is Lakeway I love the most!*

Chapter 30

Lakeway as a Retreat

or twenty-five years, Lakeway has been my retreat and refuge. Lake, hills, and sky provide a glimpse of infinity which tells me, better than words, that the messy little problems that crowd most of our days are really nothing at all. It is at Lakeway that I regain my own peace and feeling that all is right with the world.

It is a place for me to go when I need to remember who I am. It is a place where I realize that my being is a very small speck in the immense world God provided for us. It is a place where I get my sense of balance back.

Lakeway also is a place to share. When dear friends are suffering pain or grief, and I feel impotent to help, I often say, "Let's go to Lakeway." So we go and sit for an hour or two, drinking in the vastness of the countryside. It doesn't change sorrow, but it does bring strength to try again.

Lakeway is good for happy times, too. There the grandchildren and I plant trees, take walks, find fossils, count birds, and glory in the soil and the rocks, the quiet, enduring rhythm of the sun and moon.

I bought the first house at Lakeway while we were still at the University of Texas. A year later, just before we went to Houston, I bought the lot next door.

After we moved to Rice, I often went to Lakeway from Houston, where my life had grown incredibly full of obligations and commitments. After a day at Lakeway, I returned to the rich noise and bustle of my life in Houston, still knowing who I really was, and taking up my duties with renewed joy and energy.

At that time, Mona, my dear friend, and her husband were sharing the mastership at Rice's Jones College. She was the first new Rice friend to go with me to Lakeway. Over the years, as my guest lists for parties at the President's House extended until they included the whole of the Rice community, I gradually came to meet several women I thought I'd particularly like to know better.

By the time I had identified seven or eight of these women, I had completed the second house at Lakeway. It was next door to the first one, so that I was able to invite eight or ten women to spend a weekend with me without their husbands. Half of them spent the night in one house, and half in the other.

These outings included no scheduled events, just "Would you likes." These might include, "Would you like . . .

. . . to tour the State Capitol?
. . . to ride down to the LBJ Country and take the train ride?
. . . to go to the Memorial Museum at the University?
. . . to go down to the Inn for dinner?

The first contingent to Lakeway was composed of eight fascinating and unusual women, most of them involved with Rice University. The list included some of the friends I've already described — Mona Stebbings, Carolyn Wallace, Grace Bunch, and Dorie Ellsworth — and extended as well to Lorraine Dessler, who was married to a professor of engineering, and Roberta Bale, the wife of Red Bale, the athletic director, and the wife of the director of the Navy ROTC.

Four people stayed in the second house next door and three guests stayed in the main house with me. This gave us plenty of bathrooms and lots of sleeping space. The second house was used just for sleeping. During waking hours everyone was in the house Norm and I called "our house." Both houses had front yards enclosed by wrought iron fences with no access to either driveway, but offering easy access to each house.

All of our cooking, which was limited, was done in the main house. Sessions in front of the fire included acrobatics, talking and talking and talking, and laughing and laughing and laughing.

177

The Time Has Come

I discovered these women were vastly different, and strongly individualistic, each with different opinions and perspectives, each with wonderful ideas and things to say.

The first night we ate things the guests had brought — ham, salad, rolls, potato chips and dip, and wine. For dessert we had "Gene's Specialty" (pronounced "speci *ali* ty").

STRAWBERRIES ROMANOFF

Box of fresh strawberries
Sprinkling of sugar
Vanilla ice cream
Whipped cream or Cool Whip
Grand Marnier
B&B

Take stems off strawberries. Cut berries in half, slicing into large bowl. Sprinkle a little sugar over the berries.

Mix equal parts of the liquers into a measuring cup — about ¼ cup of each — Pour over strawberries. Let marinate for one-half hour.

Spoon strawberries into bottom of brandy glasses. Over this, in layers, spoon ice cream, more strawberries, more liqueur juice, more ice cream, more strawberries. Top with whipped cream.

Eat with spoon.

*   *   *

As the months flew and I became more and more a part of Rice University, I got to know a number of women faculty members as well as the faculty wives.

One group in particular I got to know very well were the wives of the masters who lived with their families on the Rice campus.

Rice's residential college system ensures that students — freshmen as well as seniors — interact with faculty members outside the classroom. Rice has eight coeducational colleges — Baker, Brown, Hansen, Jones, Lovett, Richardson, Wiess, and Will Rice. Even students who live off-campus are members of a college. Each college has its own student government, intramural teams, judicial system, and dining facilities. Each college also sponsors parties, lectures, and programs for its own members or for the whole university.

Each master and his or her spouse (when we were at Rice all the masters were men) live in a separate house adjacent to the college where they serve as master.

The masters' wives were my neighbors and, before long, my friends. Their responsibilities were to the students in their respective colleges, where they were often called on to play the role of a surrogate parent. This was particularly true in the women's colleges. Teenage women sometimes become emotional and cry. The masters' wives are most helpful. One day several years after I moved into this campus neighborhood, my first friend, Mona Stebbings, came through my back door to have a cup of coffee.

As we sat and chatted, Mona said that some of the masters' wives had approached her concerning some of the problems related to being a master's wife and living on campus.

One of their biggest problems had to do with money. To a woman, they felt that their household budgets, coming from their husbands' salaries, could not be stretched to cover expenses for entertaining and other things they did for students. They also all felt that the term "master's wife" was not the best title for what they did. They knew, as I did, that being the wife of a master, who himself was a full professor at Rice, required that the master's wife handle many problems that arose while the master was in class or office taking care of his academic responsibilities.

Mona told me that a group of these masters' wives had come to her to see if she "would ask Mrs. Hackerman to meet with the whole group." As Mona reported, they had said, "Mrs. Hackerman seems to have her act together; maybe she can help us."

We discussed possible places to meet. Mona's first suggestion was the President's House, but I knew there would be too many interruptions there.

"How would you feel about taking all of the masters' wives to Lakeway for a retreat?" she asked.

"Let's plan it," I answered.

We finally found a date that suited most of our schedules. One of the wives, Paula Baker, was a musician and had a concert scheduled at LaGrange on the date we had set, so she came up to Lakeway the next morning.

The group who came to Lakeway included Pat Martin, Paula Baker, Mary Aramiadis, Mona Stebbings, Carolyn Minter, Julie Lewis (wife of Steve Baker), and Frances Brotzen.

The retreat lasted three days. I had gone up the day before and set up the houses. I also set up the croquet equipment. When the women arrived, we had cheese and crackers, chips and dip, and wine on the front porch.

We sipped wine, nibbled on crackers, whacked the croquet ball, and giggled a lot. As the wine level went down, the laughter decibels went up. By the time it got too dark to play croquet, we probably had consumed more alcohol per person than at any other time before.

We freshened up, then went to the Inn for dinner. After dinner we sat around the living room and talked about the problems the women perceived.

Two specific problems emerged: They felt they had no title, no name, just "wife of the master," and they didn't have enough money for simple entertaining on special occasions.

A consensus was established. They would like to be called "co-masters," and they would like a small amount of money to be budgeted for their entertainment expenses.

The next day we sat out on the wall and walked about the hills. Then we went down to the Inn for lunch and enjoyed the view over the lake. Although we felt we were accomplishing something important for Rice, we had a good time and came to know each other better.

Again, I stayed over an extra day after they left, stripped the beds, and took the laundry back to Houston.

I came away convinced that it was these women who made the college system at Rice work. I talked with Norm about the real need for the co-master title — equal title for equal work! And I suggested they needed some money to help with their household budgets.

"Well, if you think that's what we should do," he answered.

Chapter 31

The MOB

One of the most visible and distinctive organizations at Rice University is the MOB — the Marching Owl Band. In the Southwest Conference, the MOB is an anomaly. It's a crazy, inventive, adorable bunch of young people who spoof themselves, the opposing teams, current events and sometimes — memorably, one time — other marching bands.

The MOB is a favorite, of course, with Rice students, and fans from other universities often told me the MOB's halftime show was worth the price of admission.

Membership in the MOB is open to any student with a musical background and a sense of fun. This very individual outfit exists within a conference where the marching bands are taken almost as seriously as football itself — the same conference that includes the University of Texas' "Showband of the Southwest" and the smart-stepping, beautifully synchronized Texas A&M band.

For me, the MOB's "sense of fun" was mightily tested one Saturday afternoon when Rice hosted Texas A&M University.

During halftime, the MOB came out after the A&M band had strutted its stuff. The MOB has no uniforms, just what tickles the members' fancy and fits in with the theme of the day. This day the MOB took on A&M's mascot, Reveille, and its marching band. The members donned military hats and went goosestepping down the field. But the A&M Corps took offense, and rushed onto the field to defend its honor. The incident would have turned into a full-blown melee without the quick work of security people and the good offices of both A&M and Rice administrators. The food service vans were guided onto the playing field. The members of the MOB climbed into the vans and were escorted to safety.

Later, at the post-game reception, I was chagrined to find some Rice alumni had missed the point. When I tried to explain to one woman the fun of it all and that it was a joke, she announced, quite seriously, "You are un-American!"

I believe I kept my cool, though I must admit it was a worrisome situation. But I would never have advocated censoring the MOB. It was creativity at its best.

The Rice/A&M difficulty happened on a Saturday night. On Sunday, Norm left for Washington, and I manned the constantly ringing phones. A&M parents called to tell me to tell him how disgusted they were. Rice alumni called to say they would never give a dime to Rice University again.

In every case, I asked the callers to leave their names, and told them that I would pass along their messages.

The next day I sent to the Development Office the names of the Rice alumni who had called. I asked the staff to check the donor records of these people. The reply came back: None had ever given any money to Rice!

Chapter 32

Women's Athletics

ootball at Rice was not the flamboyant king it had been at the University of Texas, when the Longhorns were ranked first in the nation. But intercollegiate sports and the events surrounding them at Rice were certainly big parts of our lives and the lives of Rice students. Intercollegiate athletics in the Southwest Conference cannot be ignored by university presidents and their families, and we enjoyed this aspect of university life. Football, an autumn rite that goes with the beginning of a new academic year and the crisp days that prelude winter, brings together colleagues from other universities throughout the conference and beyond.

We hosted football brunches or suppers before or after the games at the University of Texas, then again at Rice. We traveled wherever the team went to support the Longhorns and the Rice Owls, renewing friendships and acquaintances with the people at other universities. We flew on the team plane for every away game and got to know the players as young men struggling to find their way into responsible adulthood, not just as gladiator heroes. On the Rice plane, I noticed something different. After a game, UT players got on the plane glum if they had lost, noisy and triumphant if they had won. But win or lose, the Rice players boarded the plane, ate their box suppers, then pulled out the books and started studying.

An exciting new aspect of intercollegiate sports appeared at Rice University not long after we arrived — women's participation in competition with others in the Southwest Conference.

The Time Has Come

This came about through Title IX of the Education Amendments of 1972, which prohibits sex discrimination, including exclusion on the basis of sex from noncontact team sports, in those educational institutions receiving federal financial assistance.

It meant that qualified women athletes at Rice must receive athletic scholarships. Rice complied with Title IX, and I became a cheerleader for the Women Owls. This combined two of my major interests: women's issues and the importance of sports recreation.

Physical activity has always been important to me, from my elementary school days of dodge ball, hopscotch, and rope jumping. In high school I competed in volleyball and basketball, playing forward on the basketball team that won silver and bronze medals in competition with other schools at Baltimore's Coliseum. Indeed, my children, tutored in family lore, will recall that I was playing tennis when I met Norm Hackerman.

When we first arrived at Rice, we found an active intramural sports program for women as well as men, but no intercollegiate sports for women.

Joyce Hardy of Houston was president of the Rice Alumni and an avid supporter of women's sports. She was particularly concerned that Title IX caught many universities, including Rice, without coaches or facilities for women's intercollegiate sports. It was Joyce who started the Joyce Hardy Outstanding Woman Athlete Award to honor Rice women.

When I sent word to Joyce that I would like to help in any way I could, suggesting a luncheon at the President's House for Rice women athletes, she quickly responded affirmatively, adding this wistful note, "I feel as though I'm chasing a will o' the wisp. Perhaps you will loan me your magic red tennis shoes." She was alluding to my tennis shoes with the hole in the toe that I frequently wore on campus.

I enjoyed very much hosting that luncheon for about fifty women athletes, especially talking with the young women about their hopes and plans for the future. I remember particularly one pretty young woman, who had won the first Joyce Hardy Award. She told me that women athletes, after graduation, did not have the opportunities the men basketball and football stars had to earn millions in professional sports. She planned after graduation to go to Texas A&M to earn a doctorate in animal husbandry.

As we talked, she asked me, "Does Dr. Hackerman know there are women athletes here at Rice?"

"Of course he does," I answered. "Very little goes on here that he doesn't know about."

Women's competition rearranged my schedule in the President's House. I made it a point to attend every women's intercollegiate game. These were scheduled at about 6:00 P.M. as kind of warm-up events before the men's games at 7:30 or 8:00. My friends and I often were the only spectators at the women's games. We were an enthusiastic cheering section, but some of the group had to drop out. They couldn't attend regularly because they were home cooking their husbands' dinners!

My interest in women's athletics did not go unnoticed by my husband and resulted in one of his nicest surprise gifts to me. I learned about it in a letter from Joyce Hardy, dated October 30, 1978:

> It is with a great deal of excitement and joy that I inform you of a new award to be given annually in your name to the most valuable player on the Women's Varsity Basketball Team. I know you will be most pleased to learn that Dr. Hackerman has endowed this gift to the University in your honor and in recognition of your past support and continuing interest in Women's Athletics at Rice.

I sent a copy of this letter to the senior student who had asked if Dr. Hackerman knew women athletes were at Rice. "Yes, Dr. Hackerman knows . . ." I wrote.

By 1982, Rice women were participating in six National Collegiate Athletic Association sports activities — cross country, volleyball, basketball, swimming, tennis, and indoor and outdoor track.

I was invited to speak at a banquet honoring the women athletes of Rice. After much thought, I decided I wouldn't talk strictly about athletics, but more about women's changing roles and the dynamic opportunities available to them. I wanted these young women to know how life had been for their grandmothers

185

and mothers so they would better appreciate their own current possibilities and status.

"At this time I would like to present my credentials," I began . . .

First of all and most important, I am a human being and a woman. Therefore, I have been concerned, since my late teens and before I was married, about the fact that many areas of education have been "traditionally" closed to women. I wondered about whose tradition had closed them. When I expressed the thought aloud that I would like to be an architect, everybody said, "That's no place for a woman." The "traditional" jobs were school teaching, nursing, and secretarial.

I have lived in Texas for forty-six years and learned rather quickly that if you are a married woman in Texas (I have not experienced marriage for a very long time in any other state), you could not sign your name legally on any document which required you to pay for an item such as a car, refrigerator, or a stove, without first taking it home for your husband's signature. Since my husband has been a traveler for professional reasons all of our married life, this earlier period was no exception. If I had needed to purchase a refrigerator the first year or two I was in Austin, I probably would have had to wait the two weeks it would take for him to get home from a scientific meeting out of the country or the Gordon Conference in this country.

The League of Women Voters was the only organized group for women relating to anything that had to do with government matters at that time and one of the few to this day. They present information about all the candidates running for office based on information the candidates provide on a questionnaire. This gives us the opportunity to know more about each candidate before voting. I became acquainted with a number of young women within this group who were interested, as I was, in *issues* rather than just *candidates,* and together we discussed with our state legislators our concern that we could not use our own signatures, and *only* our own, on financial documents. I am happy to report that after twenty-five years of gently nudging my Senator and Representative in the Texas State House I can now sign my name and have it accepted legally — sometimes. All of these years I have encouraged women to participate as much as they want to in the political process, but by all means they should vote. I have encouraged women to know as much as possible about their financial affairs if they are married or if they are single. I have counseled women on what they can legally do with money and how to conserve it so they will not become members of the largest group of "the poor" in this country, the elderly single women. The list is long and the years number close to forty-eight. So much for credentials.

Now to get down to legal rights of women.

During the women's equality movement of the 1970s, many individual women have made the reassuring discovery that they were not alone among women of their time in questioning the traditional role society has assigned to them. I would like you to know that this questioning is not just a contemporary phenomenon. As I searched for enterprising women through two hundred years of American history, I was delighted, and even chagrined, to find our counterparts in crinolines observing truths we thought we had been the first to perceive. These facts I share with you. I call them *where we have been. Where we came from.* As far as our legal rights are concerned, the first recorded event I have been able to find occurred in 1634 to Anne Hutchinson. Our knowledge of Anne Hutchinson is one-sided: she left no letters, no journal; no one in her family or among her followers set down a portrait of her or a description of her famous "conversations" that has come down to us. Most of our knowledge comes from the pen of the man who hated her most — John Winthrop, governor of the Massachusetts Bay Colony. "A woman of a haughty and fierce carriage," wrote Winthrop, "of a nimble wit and active spirit, and a very voluble tongue, more bold than a man, though in understanding and judgment, inferior to many women."

Mistress Hutchinson and her family did not come to Boston until 1634. By that time the Calvinist faith hardened into dogma. But Mistress Hutchinson in the meantime had come to believe in the individual's direct communion with God, and in His existence in every human being — the "Covenant of Grace." She could not submit to an orthodoxy so rigid that it denied her right to express her beliefs. She had already begun to do so on board ship during the long ocean crossing. Once in Boston she won adherents in growing numbers by her rare knowledge of healing herbs, and by her eloquence. The horri-

187

fied authorities began to hear that *groups of sixty or more, mostly women but even a few men,* were meeting at the Hutchinson home, listening to Mistress Hutchinson's theories of the "Indwelling Christ" and to her penetrating criticism of the local ministers *(Century of Struggle: The Woman's Protest Movement in the United States,* p. 10; The Belknap Press of Harvard University Press: Cambridge, Mass. © 1959, 1975 by Eleanor Flexner.)

From then on the steps toward women's legal rights were long and hard and discouraging. In 1834 the American Anti-Slavery Society was in existence. Anti-slavery petitions began flowing into Congress from all over the country and *a large portion of these came from female anti-slavery societies.* The earliest known incident of *women* factory workers striking took place at Pawtucket, Rhode Island, in 1824, when they joined the men operatives in striking against a wage cut and longer worker hours. (The 102 girls and women involved held their meetings separately from the men.)

The first strike in which women alone participated was in Dover, New Hampshire, four years later (1828). In Lowell in 1834 a nameless young woman, newly fired from her job, tossed her pokebonnet in the air down in the yard as a signal to the girls watching her to leave their looms; one of them then climbed the town pump and made ". . . a flaming Mary Wollstonecraft speech on the rights of women and the iniquities of the 'monied aristocracy' which produced a powerful effect on her listeners and they determined to have their own way, if they died for it" (Flexner, p. 55).

The way had been opened, and there were workers here and there hewing away at prejudice and law; but they were scattered and isolated from one another. Grievances, even articulate voices raised in discontent, are not enough to give birth to a reform movement. What was needed now was a sharp impetus-leadership, and above all, a program. These were achieved at the Seneca Falls Convention in 1848 *from which the inception of the women's rights movement in the United States is commonly dated.* The later 1800s set the pattern for the "traditional" jobs for women which was to last until the 1950s. Those means of employment for which women actually received some kind of salary were teachers, nurses, stenographers. The first record I have uncovered is of Catharine Beecher (1800–1878), who "was not opposed to education for women, but she wanted

Women's Athletics

them educated for their natural business which, in her mind, included the teaching of small children. She spurned material concerns, and would have been insulted at the idea that her campaign to train women teachers was intended to make the country grow richer, but that's exactly what it did . . ."

"Elementary school teaching has since become so overwhelmingly a female monopoly that it is hard to realize that there was no real evidence to support Catharine Beecher's claim that women would be better as teachers than men. The women who were teaching school in the early nineteenth century were less well paid than male schoolmasters, but every few of them could be described as better. Most were sketchily educated young women in need of quick cash who knew little more than their young pupils. And there were not enough of them." (*Enterprising Women*, pp. 67–68; W. W. Norton & Co., Inc.: New York, NY. © 1976 by Caroline Bird).

The Civil War was a national disaster, but it permanently improved the economic options of women. It forced many of them into the mainstream of economic life and created permanent women's jobs for those who wanted to stay there. Women had done men's work in the Revolutionary War, but the Civil War cut deeper into everyday life. Its effect on women was more profound because it came at a time when they were being told what they could not do.

"Incredible as it seems, military hospitals before the Civil War did not even have regular nurses. Traditionally, sick and wounded soldiers had been cared for by companions or other soldiers unfit for active duty. With so many men called up, women in both North and South volunteered to nurse the soldiers.

"One of the most determined of these was Dorothea Lynde Dix (1802–1881) a New England woman nearly sixty years old, who was nationally known as an advocate of humane treatment for the mentally ill. She had begun this crusade in 1841 when she discovered, while teaching Sunday school in a jail, that it contained women guilty only of insanity. Her eloquent 'memorials' to legislatures resulted directly in thirty-two state mental hospitals" (Bird, p. 95).

She arrived in Washington just a few days after mobilization, and proposed to Col. Robert C. Wood, acting surgeon general, that she recruit and head a nursing corps of women

189

volunteers. He and others in the War Department objected on the grounds of expense and the possibility that women would add sexual temptations and scandals to the hospital problems.

The nurses had to be women of unblemished reputation with letters of recommendation from their pastors. Their services had to be requested by hospital surgeons, who could dismiss them at any time. They were to be paid $12.00 a month, a dollar less than a private soldier, and if they wore uniforms, they would supply their own.

In 1879, a thirty-three-year-old schoolteacher opened a school to teach women how to use the new typewriting machines which were being demonstrated in stores and hotel lobbies with attractive young women at the keyboard as a sales come-on. Mary Seymour's Union School of Stenography and Typewriting at 38 Park Row in New York City was not the first business "college" to offer instruction in typewriting, but it was the first to confine its student body to women.

As she succeeded in business, Mary Seymour became a more active feminist, directing her energies into open advocacy of woman's suffrage and of the broadening of employment opportunities for women.

Enough of where we came from — suffice it to say it took 122 years of constantly working by women who sincerely believed that all women were equal to all men as human beings.

The 1970 "Women's Lib" program was carried out by a new kind of woman — one who had in that period become *allowed* to have a college education and encouraged to do so, although I can remember in 1972 a young woman from Brown College at Rice University who had just been awarded an engineering degree. She came over to tell me that she had graduated in engineering and was going into a firm where she would be one of a group doing engineering and other things. Five years later another woman on the Rice campus came to lunch and excitedly told me she was going to graduate in engineering and she had a job. The firm she was entering promised to put her name on the door as "Jane Doe, Engineer."

A group of women who were in colleges all over the country in the early 1970s were caught up in hysteria of marching, parading, shouting, burning their bras — all acts that were distinctly distasteful to most men.

190

Women's Athletics

I remember coming back from California during a time in which one of our own daughters was getting a divorce. I went out to be as helpful as possible. We had tried to find a place for her to live, and ran into landlords who said, "Take this lease and get your ex-husband to cosign it." That was only one of the situations. She had no credit — it was all in her former husband's name. I was very concerned that we were 125 years away from those beginning women, and women still were not held legally equal to men.

When I got home I lashed out at my husband, saying "when I am no longer involved with a university, I'm going to spend my time actively helping in the women's movement." He said "That's great, but for Pete's sake, tell them to quit burning their bras and do something significant." At that point, I said, "It's been over 100 years of women's movements and we never really got men's attention. You know how it is with jackasses, you have to hit them with a 2x4 to get their attention." Ladies, we now have their attention. Let's not blow it.

Now we're going to talk about women and their legal rights in the future. My advice to you, if you care about holding onto the legal rights you have in this state under the Texas Constitution (which you do not have under the Federal Constitution) is that you become aware. Look at the options you have and perhaps work toward the things you care about most, either by contributing time or money. I cannot emphasize strongly enough that you need to start now saving your money. *Money is power and power is money.*

In this country women have always had some legal rights:

1. Legally born — Birth Certificate
2. Legally married — Marriage Certificate
3. Legally dead — Death Certificate

(But for many years these were true only for white women.)

However, where *money* is concerned, women were dependent either on father or husband, and where *money* is, there is the power in the marketplace.

At the time of my early married life, women were totally dependent on their husbands. I will exclude my own husband because he was, after some education from me, encouraged to realize that women could handle money. If you are dependent

191

on someone else for your everyday existence, for your food, your clothing, and your shelter, you really, truly do not have the freedom to do many things. I'm not suggesting to any woman who is married that she needs to control the money in the family. I am only suggesting that she needs to know what money does and does not do. The first time I decided that I would "go home to mother," I realized that I had no mother to go home to, and I also realized that I needed to have some money of my own. I was able to achieve this by putting aside a dollar a week out of the grocery money. It's amazing how soon you have enough to fill your car with gasoline and go away for a day. I have three daughters, all of whom I have encouraged — even if they are married — to put away a small amount of money for themselves in case they need it. For example, $1.25 a week roughly equals $60 a year. You need $100 to start a savings account and earn interest on it. You may never need it, but it's a beginning in saving money and letting money work for you.

It was 136 years between the start of the organized women's movement and its fulfillment. The early women produced all of the real roots that the women's liberation movement of the 1970s had. Those were years of no television — up until 1950 much of the spark was spread by word of mouth, by letter, and it was slow. Much, however, was achieved during that period — women were finally allowed to vote in 1920. The women's movement of the late 1960s and 1970s was led by a different kind of woman whose words and actions were instantly seen all over the country. And these women did indeed supply the 2x4s to make the rest of the country take notice. During this period we have had amendments or laws passed which have brought women closer to equality with men.

The women's equality movement draws no line between women because of their race, color, ethnic background, land of origin or religion. We are all women and should work together to achieve equality with other human beings in this country. Personally, I feel now is the time to stop diminishing men in order to build ourselves up. We need to accept men as equal human beings; we need to work for equal pay for equal jobs. And we need to save some of that equal pay to put away so that we can help, particularly in the political process. We must become involved in political policy-making and help elect women to the State Houses, Governor's Office, Mayor's Office, City

Council and, above all, to the United States Congress. Very few women are in Congress. To participate you don't have to be on a stump campaigning, but send your money to help the person you would like to see represent you. A word of caution: Do not be fooled that because the laws in Texas empower you that you have power. The people who implement those laws often are reluctant to do so. Guard your freedom and your legal rights carefully. Push for men as partners, not antagonists, and please do it in my lifetime.

At Rice I worked for women's issues on many fronts, following my lifelong commitment to work to make my own community better in whatever way I could. When I made a speech and received an honorarium, I gave the money to the Women's Athletic Department. In return, I was richly blessed. In addition to the Most Valuable Basketball Player Award, the annual Invitational Women's Volleyball Tournament at Rice is named for me.

The Board of Trustees at Rice wanted to establish an architectural scholarship in my name. The chairman of the board asked me what restrictions or other conditions I would like to have. My answer was, "Make it for graduate women." So today there is a graduate scholarship for women called the "Gene Hackerman Graduate Scholarship for Women in the School of Architecture."

In another small but important way I encourage women professionals in all fields. When my children were little, I looked for a woman pediatrician to care for them. When I need a woman lawyer, I seek one out. I regularly support capable women seeking political office. I give regularly to Emily's List, a foundation that supports the candidacies for women throughout the country. Emily's List, giving the names of candidates and the positions they seek, from every state, is published and distributed. We can choose the ones we want to support, from our state or another state. The contribution does not have to be large. It can be as little as five or ten dollars. It all counts.

I sincerely believe that it is our duty to put our money where our mouths are.

Chapter 33

Money

Books can take you to any place you want to go, tell you how to do anything you want to do, open your eyes to ideas and insights far beyond your daily trials. But, whether we like it or not, it is *money* that is power. This is something that women have been slow to learn. Many women have thought power would come with the ballot or with beauty or by using sex astutely. Somehow women didn't pay attention to Aristotle when he wrote, "(Money) is a guarantee that we may have what we want in the future. Though we need nothing at the moment, it insures the possibility of satisfying a necessary desire when it arises."

To be truly free, one needs money, not necessarily a lot of money, but enough to be mobile and comfortable. As our children were growing up, I tried to plant the idea with them that every time they had a dollar to save some of it — even just a nickel or fifteen cents.

"Put a little aside just for yourself," I would tell them. This is especially important for girl children, who during their childbearing years may be dependent on the earnings of their husbands. The advice to put aside a little money is in no way a slap at husbands nor does it reflect a prediction that someone won't be taken care of. It is really just a recognition that money *is* power and the vehicle of freedom.

I grew up in a period of time when everybody worked, if possible. Everyone knew what the "work ethic" was. As the chil-

194

Money

dren began to grow up, I felt they needed to do something so they would know what it took to make a buck. While I believe children should have chores and responsibilities around the house, they also can learn good work habits and skills working for someone other than their parents.

When Pat was in O. Henry Junior High School, she told me she wished she had a job. I suggested that we try to find her one. Soon I learned that no one hired anyone under sixteen. Still, Pat wanted a job so she would have some money of her own. I hoped she would save it for something she really wanted.

I continued to inquire around among my friends about a job for Pat, but was always turned down. It was not legal for employers to *hire* a child, even for the summer. So this devious mother made arrangements with Connelly Florists, then located at 19th Street (now Martin Luther King Blvd.) near the university for Pat to work there three mornings a week.

Pat earned thirty-five cents an hour and worked three days a week. Mrs. Hillin, the manager, gave Pat $3.15 each Friday in an envelope. At the end of the month, she sent me a bill for Pat's salary. This made Pat's employment legal, since her mother was paying her salary.

Through this experience Pat learned how good it feels to have money she had earned. (She didn't learn that I paid the salary until years later.) She also learned that having a job isn't downhill all the way. Her tasks included sweeping out the shop, making simple flower arrangements, and wrapping paper around potted plants. She did complain in late summer when the crickets came to town, as they always do in Austin in the summer. When Pat swept out the flower shop those days, the broom pushed piles of crickets away from the door.

As I had hoped, Pat did save her money. She blew it all at one stop — a shoe store, where she bought several pairs of high-heeled shoes!

Later Pat worked at the Cadeau on Guadalupe Street. She applied for and was hired for this job on her own, which was the point of the whole exercise — to give her enough confidence in her ability to work and enough self-esteem to know she would be appreciated by an employer.

195

The Time Has Come

Boys could be independent newspaper carriers long before they were sixteen years old, and Steve delivered the afternoon paper in the neighborhood throughout the year. He watched Pat's enthusiasm for her flower shop job, so the summer he was thirteen, he asked me, "Do you know anybody who needs somebody?"

Not really, but I started thinking about it. Then, as always, I was building and often needed stepping stones for paths around the garden, so I often dropped by the Smith Stone Company, where concrete stones were manufactured. I talked with the proprietor there and asked if he needed an eager youngster to work during the summer.

Steve worked half a day for about six weeks that summer, beginning at 7:00 A.M. and getting off about four hours later. He lifted and stacked the concrete stones, wearing out one or two pair of heavy work gloves every week.

The financial arrangement was the same as it had been for Pat's first job.

Steve put two and two together and came out with a right answer. "Mama, if I don't get an education, is this the kind of work I'd have to do all my life?"

When Sally was old enough to work, we were living in the University of Texas President's House on Meadowbrook. She is the only one of our children who took typing and shorthand in junior high school. So when it came time for a summer job for Sally, she had some skills to offer.

Mary Jane and Lucky Hemperley lived near us, and Mary Jane is my good friend. Lucky was manager of Farm and Home Savings. I asked him if Sally could work for him during the summer under the same arrangement Pat and Steve had had.

Sally did a good job that summer filing, typing, and taking some dictation.

We were at Rice, living in Houston, when Katy's work time came. Like Pat's job for Connelly's in Austin, Katy worked for a River Oaks flower shop. They paid her and sent me a bill. Katy didn't like the job at all; they sometimes asked her to clean the toilet. I explained to her that this was something that had to be done, that it was honorable work.

Money

The next summer Katy found a job for herself and it was more to her liking. She has always loved children, so she applied for a job at the Methodist Church Day Care Center.

Working and saving money is only a part of the story of money and its power. For many years I have conducted "Know Your Money" seminars for women both in Houston and Austin. I have been saddened often as I learn how little women know about money; some have not even known how to write a check and many don't have any idea how much money their husbands make or where the money goes.

This, of course, is unwise, and should be corrected just as surely as women needed to obtain the right to vote and the right to make contracts and have credit in their own names.

For women to be able to manage their own lives when it is necessary, it is important that they understand how to budget, how to balance a checkbook, how to keep a record of how they spend their money (if such records are not kept, it is easy to waste it), how to file tax information, and how to plan for retirement.

My seminar series are free. I hold one meeting once a week for four weeks. The first covers the organization of financial affairs, wills, trusts, safe deposit boxes, records and retirement; the second, the legal status of women today and the role of women politically, including women's involvement in public policy decisions; the third meeting covers where to put savings — certificates of deposit, MMDA, money market funds, stocks and bonds, real estate, precious metals, tax shelters, and so on; and the fourth meeting deals with taxes, insurance, and credit cards.

Chapter 34

The Floods of Houston

n the spring of 1985, we were making our plans to leave Rice University and return to Austin. We had spent fifteen wonderful years during Norm's tenure as president of Rice University, and the time had come to go home.

It was ironic that the day the movers came to pack for our move back to Austin, we had horrendous downpours. The floods of Houston were still with us.

I had arrived on the Rice campus in the midst of a driving rainstorm in the summer of 1970, concluding from that deluge that while I could be an Owl, I couldn't be a duck. Soon I learned that rain is no stranger to Houston and must always be considered in one's plans.

During our fifteen-year sojourn in the President's House at Rice we had three different floods, each of which took extraordinary measures to overcome. All three of these events bound me closer to Rice and the wonderful people who were there.

The first flood came after Sally and Dennis were married. Sally and her friend Debbie Genascol had gone to San Antonio while their husbands took the two-day Medical Board examination. Dennis had Air Force orders to report to Walter Groh Air Force Base in the Washington area as soon as he completed his medical exams. Dennis and his friend Jerry were taking the tests at the old Shamrock Hotel, about ten blocks from the Rice campus.

We were having a series of rainstorms, one piled on top of

the other. The radio and television weather broadcasters were warning motorists to avoid low places, that flooding was imminent.

That evening, just at dark, I heard Addie Mae talking to someone at the back door. "Get out of those wet clothes," she was saying. At the back door were Dennis and Jerry. They were a bedraggled sight, both sopping wet, and Jerry with a black plastic garbage bag wrapped around his leg.

When the two men had emerged from their examinations, they discovered that Dennis' car, which had been parked at the Shamrock Hotel, was under water up to the windows. Dennis and Jerry had proceeded to walk to the President's House. They had taken off their sodden shoes, and Jerry had stepped on some broken glass on the street, cutting his foot. The men stopped off at the University of Texas Medical Center on the way, and an intern friend cleaned Jerry's wound and sewed up his foot. The intern also provided the plastic garbage bag to protect Jerry's foot from further harm.

Addie Mae scurried around, found some of Norm's pajamas, and got Dennis and Jerry out of their wet things. She put the clothes in the dryer, and with the help of her magic iron, pressed the clothes back to presentability.

Dennis was particularly concerned about his car. It was the vehicle that was to take Sally and him to Washington, and which was to pull their belongings in a U-Haul trailer.

By morning the floodwaters had subsided, and, amazingly, when Dennis turned the ignition key, the engine responded. He drove the car to Rice, took out all the seats, and left the doors open to dry out the car.

The next morning Sally and Dennis left for Washington and their new adventure.

Norm was away during each of the three floods at Rice. This was the period during which he was chairman of the National Science Board and was in Washington every Thursday through Sunday. By the time of our second flood, Addie Mae had remarried and moved out of the President's House. On this particular day, Addie Mae had gone home early because of the flood warnings. When she left, it was still raining.

The Time Has Come

The power went off and left the house in darkness. Since I always have candles with globes, like hurricane lamps, handy, I had some light.

I was sitting at the kitchen table by a window, watching the weather, when I noticed water coming in through the back door. I had converted the utility room into my office. Vinyl tile had been laid in the office and down an eight-foot-long hall leading to the kitchen. Vinyl also covered the kitchen floor and went through a swinging door into a serving kitchen. At the end of this serving kitchen, however, the vinyl ended and the pile carpet began in the dining room on the other side of a swinging door.

I watched with growing dismay as that middle-sized spot of water coming under the kitchen door kept getting larger and larger and deeper and deeper. It covered my office, and crept down the hall into the kitchen. By the time it had reached the door to the serving kitchen, water was over the toes of my shoes. I began to worry in earnest about the carpets.

I went upstairs, took all the extra bedspreads and towels out of the closets, and put them at the kitchen door and at the dining room door. I felt like "the sorcerer's apprentice," or Hans with his finger in the dike, keeping Holland from being flooded.

The telephone rang. I didn't know if it was dangerous to answer a phone while standing in water, so I moved a chair to the telephone and stood on it.

Steve was calling.

"Mama," he said, "I lost my car. It stalled when I came off the Southwest Freeway at Shepperd. I turned under the freeway and water began running into it. I got out and left the car."

Steve said he had begun walking home, but decided Rice was nearer, so he would walk to the campus.

"I'll be there in about fifteen minutes."

He had called from a family's house on Shepperd. The family had lent him a raincoat.

In a few minutes Steve arrived. He got out of his wet clothes, into a pair of Norm's pajamas.

I put a tablecloth on the kitchen table, pulled out a bottle of wine, and made peanut butter sandwiches. Steve and I ate and drank by candlelight, laughing and talking about the weather and of Houston as Venice without gondolas.

The third flood I experienced at Rice affirmed that university as a special place. The founders had succeeded in stamping their institutional brainchild with the spirit of elegance, of *savoir faire,* which follows most of its graduates throughout their lives.

This flood was preceded by eight inches of rain in one downpour. Virtually everything was flooded in the colleges. Elevators didn't work; many of the telephones were out. The water around the President's House was calf-high. Rice Memorial Center, which served as the student union, and was used for large parties and for speaking engagements, was without power.

The Memorial Center was only a half mile from Shepperd Street, a main thoroughfare for Houston traffic. At 5:00 in the evening, high traffic time, the rain was still coming down and dozens of cars were being flooded and stalled on Shepperd. These flood victims were abandoning their cars and walking to the center to get in out of the wet and let their families know (thinking there would be telephone service) they wouldn't be home for a while.

Marion Hicks, director of food service at Rice, opened up the dining area at Memorial Center for the refugees. Since the telephone in the President's House was the only one working on campus, Mr. Hicks sent a student waiter into the rain to tell me a lot of people were stranded at the center with no way to get messages to their families. He sent me the names and home numbers of several people and asked if I'd make these calls.

After I had done this, I put on my rubber boots, got out my umbrella and sloshed through the water to the Memorial Center.

I found fifty or sixty people there. Mr. Hicks had laid the cloth tablecloths and set the tables with the silver candelabra. He was slicing canned turkey and ham while several students made the sandwiches by candlelight. I asked if I could help, and he said, "If you want to make sandwiches, come on." I did.

After a time, Mr. Hicks invited our guests: "Come on," he said, "the food is ready."

At every place Marion Hicks had laid a knife, fork and spoon, and napkin.

201

The Time Has Come

From that moment on, I was absolutely committed to Rice University.

After this third flood, Norm decided something permanent had to be done, so a new drainage system was installed under the campus. This didn't stop Houston's enveloping rains, but it did keep the campus from flooding.

*   *   *

And now we were getting ready to move on, complete with damp, but not quite rain-soaked, boxes. My destination was Austin. As I drove northward, I sang: "Austin, Austin, here I come, right back where I started from."

Chapter 35

You Can Go Home Again

s I pulled into the driveway at the townhouse we owned in Austin, I felt a great wave of joy. The rains on the coast had not reached us yet, and the warm June sun made all the potted plants on my deck appear to be smiling at me. I sat out there for some time, listening to the water of the little creek flowing under the deck, enjoying a sense of peace as I said to myself, "We did it. We did it. For fifteen years we did it."

As I sat there on the deck, Mona and Ronald Stebbings' son and his wife, who live in Austin, arrived with a caterer's tray of cold cuts and salads for my first dinner back home.

One of my friends, Mary Nell Garrison, had sent me a note while I was still in Houston saying she had read in the paper that Norm and I would be returning to Austin in July and that they were going to "shoot off fire crackers!"

And so they did — on the Fourth of July (as Austin usually does). I was invited by Tom and Betty Morgan to watch the display above the river from the top floor of the Headliners Club.

I slipped back into my community life with ease, seeing old friends, attending parties, and looking at houses to buy. The results were the usual. I found a house, I rebuilt the house, and later put a second story on the house.

At that point our fiftieth wedding anniversary was upon us.

Chapter 36

Once More to Staten Island

The year was 1990; the month was September; and the Middle Atlantic states were sweltering in a giant Turkish bath. My husband of fifty years and I were enjoying a trip to New York that our grown-up children had planned as an anniversary gift.

They asked me what I wanted to do in New York. Perhaps they thought I'd want to shop or go to the Metropolitan Museum, or to Carnegie Hall, all the things I had wanted to do on other trips to the city.

Not this time. This time, I told them, "I want to ride the Staten Island Ferry, then the bus, getting off at the stop on Richmond Road. I want to find the house where Norm and I lived when we were first married . . ."

And so we did. I approached the trip with a schoolgirl's anticipation, and thankfulness that Norm and I could share this walk into the past and the search with our children for our beginnings together.

Our four children and their spouses came with us to New York — Pat with her husband, Mike Berry; Steve with his wife, Mary; Sally with her husband, Dennis Myers; and Katy and her husband, Brian Gaffney.

Mike and Dennis had business to attend to in New York and couldn't take the whole morning to go with us to Staten Island, so only eight of us went on this expedition. Every time we went anywhere in the city, we had to engage two taxicabs. Moving eight

204

people around in separate cabs was time-consuming. Two cab drivers didn't use the same routes *ever,* whatever the destination.

The cab I took from the hotel arrived first at the ferry. At the dock, we learned that we had a half-hour wait for the next ferry.

In New York City, every place you look some kind of food is for sale — hot dogs, hot bagels, sweet rolls, cups of coffee, Orange Juliuses. And our family gets hungry at virtually every hour of the day. Every time I looked around, someone had gone to get something *else* to put in their mouths.

Steve was the tour director, so he was busy getting the exact change in quarters we needed for the ferry. He was hustling quarters while I was worrying about the other taxicab, carrying the rest of our group. I was afraid we would miss the ferry departure. Finally, the second cab arrived, and everyone piled out a half-block away in the middle of the street and rushed over to join us at the covered dock.

Of course, they were hungry, too!

The day was a little hazy, but we could clearly see the Statue of Liberty and Ellis Island in the distance. It was Saturday and the ferry was not full. It was still early, before 9:00, so the tourists hadn't gotten there yet.

We talked about the place Norm and I had lived. I knew the name of the street — Richmond Road. Norm didn't remember that, but, amazingly, he remembered the number of the house, 2170.

Unerringly, we found the bus stop, the same place I had waited for the bus fifty years ago. Here again the problem of exact change or bus tokens came up. New Yorkers are wonderful. We had conversations with a variety of people about bus tokens, and they generously sold tokens to us. Pat took videotape of our new friends, and we will remember them always, whenever we look at the video of our trip. Pat recorded the entire trip with her camcorder.

We had a twenty-minute wait for the Richmond Road bus. The bus driver told us the 2100 block was across the street from the cemetery, and I remembered he was right.

Until we all got together on the bus, I hadn't realized that our family talks *all* the time. They not only talk *all* the time, but *all at the same time.* It was a continuing celebration of laughter and talk, with everyone stumbling over each other to get words out or quips in. The bus driver seemed to sigh with gratitude when we got off.

All the time my excitement, tinged with a bit of dread (what if the house wasn't there?), was putting a lump in my throat. When we got off the bus, we were looking at a block-long row of connected brick duplexes. THEY WERE THERE!

We came to 2170.

"That's it!" I shouted to Norm.

"No, it can't be," he said. "This is a newer building."

"Yes, it is. Yes, it is." I looked up at the window. "That's where I did my typing for Dr. Hallquest. I'm sure that's it."

The houses are built on a kind of rise. Each has a little porch, like a stoop, with two doors opening from it — one door leading to the apartment right there, and the other opening to stairs that lead to the apartment upstairs. It was just like it had been fifty years ago.

Pat walked with me down the sidewalk and around the row of houses into the back alley. Our house was in the middle of the block. I gave another cry of recognition and delight. Clothes were hanging on the line! This was it. The memories came crowding over me, washing clothes in the deep sink in the kitchen, then hanging them on the line that operated from a pulley at the window near the sink.

The duplexes were showing their ages in the back. Apparently, the front facade had been refurbished.

Here came a man carrying a sack of trash. "Do you live here?" we asked him.

"No, I'm the real estate agent. Why are you taking pictures?"

"My husband and I lived here fifty years ago. Is this the same apartment house?"

"Yes," he answered. "A woman who lived in the end apartment told me she had lived here for fifty years. She just moved out last week, so the houses were here fifty years ago. These are the same ones."

Once More to Staten Island

Meanwhile, Pat had struck up a conversation with a young woman entering the door. Pat told her that we had lived there when we were first married. The woman said she lived upstairs. Pat said her mother and father had lived downstairs. Since the apartments were identical the woman asked us if we wanted to see hers.

Pat and I went with her up the stairs. Incredibly, it was just as it had been. Pat took pictures of it for the others to see.

"Mom, here's the bus," one of the children called. And so it was.

I hesitated and turned to capture again the tall, blonde girl who had walked in and out of that door — the young woman who had begun here the long and happy marriage with Norman Hackerman.

This fish didn't get away! A memento from Steve Hackerman's fishing trip with his mother.
— Photo from Hackerman Collection

Pat, Steve, and Sally Hackerman greet their mother when Gene Hackerman returns home from work at the Texas Legislature.
— Photo courtesy of *Austin American-Statesman*

208

Gene Hackerman with Mrs. James Colvin and Vice President Colvin, greeting a guest at a University of Texas reception, 1961.
— Photo courtesy of University of Texas at Austin

The Hackermans exchange pleasantries with the James Dolleys in University of Texas receiving line. Dr. L. D. Haskew is at left.
— Photo courtesy of University of Texas at Austin

A typical University of Texas at Austin receiving line in the 1960s. From left: Mrs. Raymond Vowell and Vice Chancellor Vowell, Mrs. Wilson Stone and Vice Chancellor Stone, Mrs. L. D. Haskew and Vice Chancellor Haskew, Mrs. Norman Hackerman and President Hackerman (back to camera), Mrs. James Dolley and Vice Chancellor Dolley, Mrs. W. W. Heath and Chairman of the University System Board of Regents Heath, and Chancellor Harry Ransom and Mrs. Ransom.

— Photo courtesy of University of Texas at Austin

Mrs. James Colvin and University of Texas Vice President Colvin and Mrs. Norman Hackerman and President Hackerman in receiving line for University of Texas faculty reception, 1968.

— Photo courtesy of News and Information Service, University of Texas at Austin

Mrs. Norman Hackerman with Mrs. C. J. Oliver and Mrs. Preston Smith at the Texas Governor's Mansion.

— Bill Malone photo

Gene Hackerman working at her desk in the University of Texas President's House on Meadowbrook Drive in Austin.

— Photo courtesy of *Rice Review*

Gene Hackerman works with her secretary, Virginia Carr, in the family room of the University of Texas President's House on Meadowbrook Drive in 1970. The Hackermans hosted many events at the Meadowbrook house for university faculty, students and administrators.

— Photo courtesy of *Rice Review*

Gene Hackerman in her office at the University of Texas President's House on Meadowbrook Drive in Austin. Mrs. Hackerman has had an office in every Texas house she has lived in, beginning with a curtained-off space in the garage at 2000 Sharon Lane.

— Photo courtesy of
Rice Review

Gene Hackerman in 1970 cuddles Chris Hackerman, son of Steve and Mary Hackerman.

— Photo courtesy of *Rice Review*

Katy Hackerman at the piano and Sally Hackerman with the guitar receive some impromptu praise for their music-making from their mother.

— Photo courtesy of *Rice Review*

213

The Hackerman family together in the garden at the University of Texas President's House on Meadowbrook Drive in 1970, just before they moved from Austin to Houston and Rice University. From left: Steve, Katy, Gene with Chris, Norman, Mary, and Sally. — Photo courtesy of *Rice Review*

Gene, Norman, Mary Hackerman with Chris, son of Mary and Steve Hackerman.
— Photo courtesy of *Rice Review*

214

The four Hackerman children in 1961: Pat (holding Katy), Steve, and Sally.
— Photo from Hackerman Collection

Gene Hackerman with Mrs. Lyle Gilbertson and Mrs. Ray Hurd at Electrochemical Society meeting in Houston.

— W. D. Murdy photo

During the summer of 1970, Gene Hackerman worked with architect Robert Folsom Lent and James P. Berling of Rice University on plans to enlarge and remodel the existing President's House on the Rice University campus.
— Photo courtesy of Rice University

Chairman of the Rice University Board of Governors Malcolm Lovett (right) presents Dr. Norman Hackerman with a summons to his inauguration as president of Rice University in 1971. Members of Dr. Hackerman's family look on. From left: Pat, Mary, Chris, Gene, Katy, and Sally.
— Photo courtesy of Houston Chronicle

University of Houston President Philip Hoffman and Mrs. Hoffman with Gene and Norman Hackerman at Cougar Club party in Houston, September 9, 1972.

— Photo courtesy of University of Houston

Faculty reception at Rice University in September 1973. From left: Fletcher Brown and Katherine Tsanoff Brown, Gene and Norman Hackerman, Mrs. Sam Jones, and Dean Sam Jones of the Shepherd School of Music.

— Photo courtesy of Rice University

217

Dr. Margaret Mead with President Hackerman before her address at a Rice Associates Dinner in spring 1975. Dr. Mead's subject was "A New Dynamic for Higher Education."

— Photo courtesy of *Houston Chronicle*

President Hackerman introduces author James Michener, speaker at a Rice Associates Dinner on March 21, 1984.

— Photo courtesy of Rice University

Walter Cronkite, Anne Duncan, and Charles Duncan with Gene and Norman Hackerman at Rice Associates Dinner in 1982.

Dr. and Mrs. Norman Hackerman with Prince Philip, the Duke of Edinburgh, in the Rice University President's House at a luncheon during a symposium in Houston co-sponsored by Rice University and the World Wildlife Fund, November 5, 1982.

— Photo courtesy of Rice University

Dr. Norman Hackerman with Dr. Henry Kissinger, Josephine Abercrombie, vice chairman of the Board of Governors of Rice University, and Mrs. Hackerman. Dr. Kissinger spoke at a Rice Associates Dinner.
— Photo courtesy of Rice University

A luncheon for women athletes at Rice University President's House. Both President Hackerman (center, front) and Mrs. Hackerman (top of her head showing at second table) worked to encourage a wide array of women's athletics at Rice.
— Photo courtesy of Rice University

220

Addie Mae Patterson and Sally Hackerman on the occasion of Pat Hackerman's marriage in Houston to Dr. Michael Berry.

— Family photo

Elizabeth Meyers dancing with her cousin Chris Hackerman at Katy Hackerman's wedding to Brian Gaffney.

— Photo courtesy of Heinz Kugler

Dr. and Mrs. Hackerman with Jack Josey, president of the Welch Foundation.
— Family photo

Gene Hackerman in conversation with Dr. Glenn T. Seaborg, Nobel Laureate, at Welch Foundation dinner. — Photo courtesy of Welch Foundation

222

Gene Hackerman and Josephine Abercrombie, vice chairman of the Board of Governors of Rice University, at a Houston Country Club luncheon, April 1985. At this luncheon Mrs. Abercrombie announced the naming of the annual Rice Women's Volleyball Tournament for Mrs. Hackerman and the founding of a new scholarship – the Gene C. Hackerman Scholarship in Architecture for a graduate woman student.

— Photo courtesy of Rice University

Mrs. George Brown (left) with former President Lyndon B. Johnson and Mrs. Hackerman at the dedication of Richardson College, Rice University, October 16, 1971.
— Photo courtesy of Rice University

Bernard and Ann Sakowitz with Gene and Norman Hackerman.
— Lieber photo

Index

Index

227

KTBC-Radio, 54, 130
KTBC-TV, 54, 136

L

Lakeway, 175, 176-177
Land Grant Colleges and Universities, 132
LBJ Library, 111
LBJ Ranch, 110, 136
LBJ School of Public Affairs, 137
League of Women Voters, 186
Lee, Gypsy Rose, 7
Lester, Paul, 20
 Sylvia, 19, 64
Lewis, Julie, 180
Lieberman, Joe, 110
 Rita, 110
Liedtke, Betty, 97
 Hugh, 97
Lindbergh, Anne Morrow, 123
Longhorn Band, 117
Lovett, H. Malcolm, 139, 143
 H. Malcolm, Jr., 140
 Malcolm Odell, 140, 143
 Martha, 157
Loving, Maribel, 38

M

M.D. Anderson Hospital, 65, 68-69, 108, 134
McBee, Sue Brandt, 53, 55
McCann, Mr., 102
McCauley, —, 63, 65, 66, 77-78
MacCorkle, Lucille, 19-20
McKetta, Johnnie, 65
McReynolds, Dr., 169
Maguire, Jack, 146
 Pat, 89
Martha Ann Zivley's Typing Service, 37
Martin, Pat, 180
Mary Seymour's Union School of Stenography and Typewriting, 190
Mason, Jack, 48
Massachusetts Institute of Technology, 59
Matsen, Al, 18, 23
 Ceil, 18-19, 23, 64

Megan, 20
Ricky, 18, 20, 23
Maurer, Jean, 19, 20, 64
 Joanna, 20
Mead, Margaret, 96
Meniere, Mr., 31
Methodist Church Day Care Center, 197
Methodist Church Headquarters, 1
Metropolitan Museum, 4
Michener, James, 96
Minter, Carolyn, 188
Moore, Bernice "Bunk," 67, 73, 116
 Harry, 67
Morgan, Betty, 203
 Tom, 203
Morris, Truman, 23
Morrison, Tinker, 134
Morton, Robert, 108
Most Valuable Basketball Player Award, 193
Music Corporation of America (MCA), 113
Myers, Dennis, 82, 198, 204
 Evelyn, 35, 78
 Jack, 35, 78
 Sally Hackerman, 198, 204 (see Sally Hackerman)

N

National Collegiate Athletic Association, 185
National Council on the Arts, 135
National Science Board, 199
National Science Foundation, 137, 161
Nelson, Agnes, 60
New York City, 4, 205
New York Stock Exchange, 9
New York University, 3
1940 World's Fair, 7
Nixon, Mr., 35
 Richard, 138
Nixon-Clay Business College, 32, 34, 36
Norfolk and Western Railroad, 12
Norton, Carolyn, 14
 Mr., 13

Index

Nugent, Luci Johnson, 138
  Lyndon, 138
  Pat, 138

O
O. Henry Junior High School, 195
Olan, Levi, 82
Old Brown Owl, 48
Old Dallas Highway, 17
"Old Owl Hoots, The," 48

P
Parent-Teacher Association, 115
Patterson, Addie Mae, 63, 65, 76,
  101, 102, 106, 121, 134, 146,
  160-161, 171, 199
Peace Corps, 52
Pearl Harbor, 11, 12
Peck, Gregory, 112, 114
Peterson, Roger Tory, 157
Piccadilly Cafeteria, 18
Pilzer, Kenneth, 139
Pittman, Russ, 160
Pomphret Manor, 60
Powers, John Robert, 5-6
Prince Philip, 155-157
Princeton University, 109
Pryor, Cactus, 54, 111

Q
Quay, Bill, 54

R
Radio House, 46
Reddick, DeWitt, 41
Reveille, 181
Revell, Owen, 28
Revell Interiors, 28
Rice Chapel, 83
Rice Memorial Center, 201
Rice's Jones College, 177
Rice University, 87-88; Alumni Asso-
  ciation, 167; Board of Gover-
  nors, 144; Board of Trustees,
  95, 139; colleges, 178; football,
  183; Marching Owl Band, 181-
  182; presidency, 139; president,
  111; President's House, 139-147,
  158; president's wife, 95-98;
  women's athletics, 184-193
Riesman, David, 88

Roanoke Hotel Dining Room, 12
Roberdeau Storage, 16
Robinson, Anne, 79
  Harold, 79-80
Roessner, Roland, 132
Roosevelt, Teddy, 138
Rosenthal, Pat Hackerman, 121 (*see*
  Pat Hackerman)
  Ray, 122-123, 125, 127
  Wendy, 121, 175

S
St. David's Church, 66
Salisbury, Harrison, 96
San Antonio Zoo, 59
Sandburg, Carl, 1
Sanford, Agnes, 67
  Fillmore, 51-52
Scarbrough's Department Store, 33
Scarbrough's Foundations Depart-
  ment, 107
Schiwetz, Buck, 92, 93
Scottish Rite Dormitory, 34
Scrub Scouts, 49
Seneca Falls Convention in 1848,
  188
"separate but equal," 30
Seton Hospital, 63-64, 69, 79, 81,
  103, 134
Seventh District Conference of
  Parents and Teachers, 55
Seymour, Mary, 190
Shakespeare Festival, 42
Shanks, Louis, 142
Shepherd School of Music, 152
Shepherd Society, 154
Simenon, Georges, 125
Simon, William, 96
Simpson, Adele, 4-6
Sims, —, 76
Smiley, Joseph, 103
Smith Stone Company, 196
Sontag, Beverly, 67
  Jim, 67
  Paul Bolton, 67, 131
Southern Union Gas Company, 23
Southwest Texas State Teachers
  College, 136
Spelce, Neal, 130

229

230